LONDON LIVERY COMPANY APPRENTICESHIP REGISTERS

VOLUME 15

GOLD AND SILVER WYRE DRAWERS' COMPANY 1693-1837

abstracted and indexed by Cliff Webb

1998

Published by
Society of Genealogists
14 Charterhouse Buildings
Goswell Road
London EC1M 7BA

© C R Webb 1998

ISBN 1 85951 084 1

TABLE OF CONTENTS

Table of contents	iii
General introduction to series	v
Gold and Silver Wyre Drawers' Company apprenticeships	v
Index of apprenticeships	1
Index of masters	29
Index of places	33
Index of subjects	39

GENERAL INTRODUCTION TO SERIES

The records of the Livery Companies of London are one of the greatest archival treasures of the world. Dating from the early medieval period to the present, they provide a mass of information for a variety of historians of innumerable subjects. For the family historian, they can provide an immense amount of genealogical and biographical details about their members.

A large proportion of these records are now deposited at the Guildhall Library, where they may be freely and conveniently consulted. Again, from the genealogical viewpoint, the two most important series of records tends to be those where people were apprenticed to a master, and those where individuals were admitted as freemen of the company in question.

In early records, persons who belonged to a given Livery Company would generally practice the trade to which that Company referred, but after about 1650, it became more and more common (until in some companies virtually universal) that members practiced another trade altogether. Searchers, therefore, even if they know the occupation of the subject of interest, may not be able to find the right Livery Company to search at all easily. By no means all those apprenticed went on to become freemen. Some died, some left their masters before their term expired and others while completing their apprenticeship simply never took up the freedom to which they were entitled. On the other hand, not all becoming free had been apprenticed. Sons of freemen (born when the father was free) were entitled to freedom 'by patrimony' and in most companies you could simply buy the freedom 'by redemption'. Freedom by redemption, indeed, became commoner and commoner during the latter part of the eighteenth century, and Livery Company records tend to become less interesting. For this reason it was decided that the priority should be to calendar apprenticeship records rather than freedom admissions.

This series is designed to provide family and other historians with the information provided by the records of apprenticeship of a number of the Livery Companies. Series have been selected from those companies whose apprenticeship records generally give good genealogical detail, principally, the name, parish and occupation of the apprentice's father. The records have been sorted into alphabetical order of apprentice, and supplemental indexes provided of masters, places and occupations. Generally, the work of abstraction will end about 1800, though generally abstraction will be to the end of a manuscript volume.

There are two alternate general sources for limited periods for London apprenticeships. Firstly, the original papers supporting a granting a freedom from apprenticeship survive in the Corporation of London Record Office from 1681. Though often very difficult to use - they were strung together through a hole in the middle - they are invaluable for companies whose records do not survive, or for which only undetailed records are extant. From 1710 until 1814, there was a duty on apprenticeship, and the records of this are preserved in the Public Record Office. Until about 1750, the father's name, parish and occupation are given, and there are a series of indexes for the period 1710 to 1774 at the Society of Genealogists. There were, however, a large number of exemptions under this act, and naturally as many people as possible sought this exemption, and so many apprenticeships which might be expected to be found in this index are not there. It is, again, however, an invaluable substitute, if partial, for lost records and as a general index and lucky dip.

The abstracts are generally limited to the name of the apprentice, his father's name, parish and occupation, the name of the master and the date of the indenture. If the record notes that he was subsequently turned over to another master, or, as is sometimes recorded, became free, died etc. this has also been noted. Details such as the street in which the master lived, the term of apprenticeship (usually seven years, but occasionally shorter or longer) and the premium paid have been omitted.

GOLD AND SILVER WYRE DRAWERS' APPRENTICESHIPS

The records of this company are deposited at the Guildhall Library. The company obtained its charter in 1693. A single apprenticeship register (Guildhall Library Ms 2455) covers all the apprenticeships from 1693 to 1837. This index covers all these records.

Almost all the early entries in the register contain a 'turn over' from an official of the company. These have been ignored in the text, and only the 'real' master has been noted where the 'turn over' is simultaneous with the original binding. However, these early masters are almost universally members of another livery company, presumably because there were few people free of this company, so recently founded. The normal 'conventional' master from 1693 to 1700 was Richard Brady, from 1700 to 1721 George Meakins, from 1722 to 1734 John Leech, from 1734 to 1740 Richard Drury, after a gap from 1746 to 1760 by Robert Wrathall and after another gap by James Dennis from 1769 to 1788. The last such entry is the apprenticeship of William Lewis (11 Sep 1788). These masters' names have been omitted from the text of this index. After the 1740s there are few of these entries, as almost all apprentices were apprenticed immediately to their real intended master. The masters not of the Gold and Silver Wyre Drawers' were chiefly of the Blacksmiths', Goldsmiths', Grocers', Longbowstringmakers', Merchant Taylors' or Weavers' Companies.

Perhaps because of this small size, some masters are annotated in the form 'one of this company, citizen and vintner'; for an example, see the apprenticeship of Thomas Eades in 1728.

Until 1726 (and for three entries in 1820) the register is annotated 'F' or 'dead' in the margin of many entries. 'F', of course, signifies that the apprentice later took the freedom of the company. In this index <free> and <dead> (after the date) have been used to denote these sorts of entries.

There are records of 1,261 apprenticeships in these Gold and Silver Wyre Drawers' records.

Cliff Webb. January 1998.

GOLD AND SILVER WYRE DRAWERS' APPRENTICESHIPS

Abbisdiston Jonas s Jonas, Holborn, cordwainer† to Thomas Atwood 9 Sep 1725
Abell Mathew s Mathew, Atherstone, War, tanner to James Gramar 16 Aug 1722 <free>
Acritt Robert s John, White Cross Street, spinner to Elizabeth Gantum, member of this company,
　citizen and goldsmith 11 Nov 1725
Adams John s William, Holborn, Mdx, surgeon† to George Callisse, citizen and haberdasher
　21 Jul 1714
Adams Richard s Richard, Aldgate, Lnd, smith to Nicholas Pingstone 4 Apr 1793
Adams William s William, Worcester, Wor† to John Swaine 6 Mar 1715/6
Adey William George s Thomas, Old Kent Road, gentleman to Thomas Pell Atkinson 7 Feb 1825
Ailesbury Andrew s Thomas, Mells, Som, clothier to Thomas Newton turned over to John Ferrys
　14 Feb 1722/3
Ainsworth Rowland s George, citizen and haberdasher to Evan Worsley,
　citizen and longbowstringmaker 7 Oct 1708
Alcraft Henry s Thomas, citizen and cutler to Richard Cooke 29 Aug 1728
Aldred Henry s Samuel Higham to Samuel Botson Aldred 11 Aug 1824
Alexander Walter Corner s John, St Luke, Mdx, locksmith to John Drake 11 Sep 1735
Alexander William s John to Thomas Collins 10 Oct 1754
Allen Joseph s David to Robert Wrathall 9 Apr 1752
Allson Thomas s William, Sevenoaks, Ken, yeoman to Thomas Brock, citizen and merchant tailor
　23 Jun 1708 <free>
Allsup Charles s Thomas, Boyleston, Dby, clerk to Henry Southouse 13 Nov 1697 <dead>
Alston John s Samuel, citizen and merchant tailor† to Richard Drury 7 Jun 1705 <free>
Anderton Uriah s Edward, citizen and dyer to William Harker 1 Nov 1711 <9 Dec 1714
　turned over to Nicholas Cunliffe; free>
Andrews Thomas s Richard, Beech Lane, Lnd, carpenter to Samuel Roberts 9 Dec 1779
　<10 Jun 1784 turned over to Benjamin Roberts>
Appleford Henry Johnson s John, Hammersmith, Mdx, cordwainer to John Edenbury 16 Jul 1804
Appleford John Henry s Henry Johnson to his father 26 Jul 1830
Arch John s Giles, citizen and cordwainer† to Robert Questwood, citizen and broderer 30 May 1701
Archer Robert s George† to Joseph Atkinson 15 Aug 1755
Armour Thomas s William, New Crane, Wapping, Mdx, victualler to Charles Dodsworth,
　citizen and weaver 8 Aug 1728
Arnold John s William, White Cross Street, Lnd, bricklayer to John Read 8 Mar 1781
Arrowsmith John s John, Westminster, Mdx, gentleman to Thomas Wells, citizen and broderer
　24 Feb 1701/2
Ash Robert s Edward, St George in the East, Mdx, yeoman to Daniel Atherley 9 Jun 1774
Ashford Edmund Francis s Edmund, Clerkenwell, Mdx, bookbinder† to Thomas Cowald
　9 Dec 1784
Ashmead John s Thomas, St Olave Southwark, Sry, distiller to William Dark,
　citizen and merchant tailor 15 May 1707 <free>
Ashton Walter s Walter, gold & silver wyre drawer to Thomas Chandler 12 Nov 1717 <free>
Aspin John s John, Sharps Alley, Smithfield, wheelwright to John Smith, citizen and weaver
　9 Aug 1733
Atherfeild Eleanor d William, Sundridge, Ken, yeoman to John Leech turned over to John Dunne,
　citizen and goldsmith 10 Sep 1730
Atherfold William s George to John Jones 13 Nov 1760
Atkins William Henry s Michael Thomas, Clerkenwell, Mdx to William Walker 2 Jul 1822
Atkinson Christopher s Amy to Henry Questeard 8 Oct 1747
Atkinson Joseph s Joseph, citizen and barber surgeon† to William Harker 14 Dec 1738
Atwood Thomas s Samuel, Charlton Abbots, Gls, yeoman to John Collins,
　citizen and merchant tailor 7 Jul 1698 <free>
Austin Jeremiah s Leonard to William Morgan 14 Nov 1751
Austin John s Marmaduke, Tottenham, Mdx, gardener to Richard Hill, citizen and haberdasher
　27 Jan 1703/4 <free>
Austin John s John to John Gifford 12 May 1743
Austin Thomas s Thomas, West Smithfield, tailor to James Reynolds 27 Jan 1820 <free>
Ayres Henry s Abraham Harry, Barking, Ess to Thomas Pell Atkinson 21 Jun 1824

1

GOLD AND SILVER WYRE DRAWERS' APPRENTICESHIPS

Baber Edward s Thomas, citizen and dyer to John Joseph 15 Aug 1709
Bagshaw John s Joseph, St Giles Cripplegate, tailor to Richard Drury 14 Feb 1733/4
Bailey John s Francis to John Farr 12 Feb 1746/7
Baily Thomas s Thomas, citizen and mason to Andrew Jellico, citizen and haberdasher 31 Jul 1701
Baker Arthur s William, citizen and dyer to Robert Berkley 9 Jul 1712
Baker John s John, citizen & grocer to Thomas Pensom, cit. & haberdasher 17 Sep 1705 <free>
Baker John s Henry, St Pauls Churchyard, Lnd, cabinet maker† to James Douglas 6 Nov 1734
Baker Thomas s Thomas, All Hallows London Wall, Lnd, cordwainer† to Joseph Carter 11 Aug 1737
Balance Thomas s Richard, citizen and cordwainer† to John Atkinson, citizen and goldsmith 22 Sep 1698 <free>
Banks William s Arthur, St John St., Clerkenwell, Mdx, shoemaker† to John Waller 14 Jan 1730/1
Banks William s William to his father 10 Sep 1761
Bardin Richard s Thomas, Hewitts Court, Charing Cross, yeoman to George Burnett 5 Sep 1792
Barker Joseph s Joseph to Thomas Edwards 14 Apr 1768
Barker Thomas s Joseph† to Walter Pert 12 Nov 1741 <9 Dec 1742 turned over to (Mr) Cunliffe>
Barkington Thomas s Edward, Old Street, cane chairmaker to Orme Quarry 11 Dec 1729
Barnard William s Thomas to Daniel Atherley 11 Sep 1766
Barnes Thomas s Elizabeth, widow to Robert Pitter 5 Jan 1748/9
Barnsley Henry s Robert, labourer† to Francis Wilkinson 8 May 1740
Barrard John Arnold s Edward, St Saviour Southwark, innholder to William Harker 7 Jan 1724/5
Barrott James s James† to George William Naylor 12 May 1757
Barrow Charles s Thomas, Lnd, gentleman† to William Thomas 18 May 1704
Barrow Charles s Thomas, St Clement Danes, Mdx, gentleman† to John Fletcher, citizen and grocer 6 Nov 1705 <free>
Barrow Joseph s Joseph, Bethnal Green, Mdx, tinplateworker to John Churchman (jnr.) 1 Sep 1828
Barrow William s Joseph to John Churchman (snr.) 27 Feb 1831
Bartington Thomas s Thomas to his father 12 Jul 1753
Barwick Thomas s Charles, Croydon, Sry, yeoman to Thomas Robert Birch 15 Aug 1807
Baseley John s John, Gravenhurst, Bdf, yeoman to William Harker 20 Mar 1704/5 <free>
Bassam William s William, citizen and merchant tailor to Richard Drury 5 Feb 1716/7
Bateman John s John, 'Houlditch Woolsington', Sal, gentleman to Thomas Price, citizen and merchant tailor 23 Dec 1697
Bates Francis s Francis† to Francis Houlton 11 Sep 1760
Batson James s John, gentleman to Messrs Henry Alcraft and Joseph Haywood 21 Oct 1742
Batson Robert s John, Fleet Street, Lnd† to Michael Paxton 28 Oct 1726
Bayes John s John, St Giles Cripplegate, Mdx, farrier to Walter Wood, citizen and hatbandmaker 31 Dec 1705 <free>
Bayley Joseph s Joseph, Effingham, Sry, labourer to Evans Worsley, citizen and longbowstringmaker 9 Jan 1706/7
Bayley Mark s John, Great Brickhill [in Ms 'Great Mickhill'], Bkm, yeoman to James Douglas, citizen and vintner 13 Mar 1705/6 <free>
Bead John s Guy† to William Goome 14 May 1761
Beale Samuel s Edward, Whitechapel, Mdx, yeoman to Thomas Chapman 8 Jun 1814
Bean James s Thomas to Henry Questead 9 Oct 1740 (St Giles Cripplegate charity)
Beane James s John, Canterbury, Ken, milliner to Alexander Parratt (jnr.) 22 Mar 1694/5
Beer John s Richard to William Goome 9 Jun 1768 and 8 Jun 1769
Becston James s George, St Luke, Mdx, jeweller to Elizabeth Gascoyne (widow) 11 Oct 1744
Belcher John Isaac s John, Hampton Court, Mdx, yeoman† to Anthony Sparrow 4 Jun 1793
Bell Alexander s Alexander† to John Macey 12 Jul 1764
Bell James Thomas David s James to Stephen Crouch 25 Oct 1824
Bell William s David, Shoreditch, Mdx, ironmonger to James Thomas David Bell 13 Apr 1837
Bellenger Adam s Francis, Thames Street† to John Winter 10 Jan 1744/5
Bencroft William s Thomas, Hungerford Market, Strand to John May 25 Jun 1829
Bennell John s William† to Robert Crew 13 Dec 1750
Bennett Charles s Joseph† to Thomas Brown 13 Sep 1750
Bennett Richard s George to Charles Lockwood 9 Mar 1769
Benning James s James, citizen and vintner† to Goodwin Washbourn 30 Mar 1708 <free>

GOLD AND SILVER WYRE DRAWERS' APPRENTICESHIPS

Bensom William s William, Lnd, citizen and merchant tailor† to William Simmonds 16 Dec 1714
Bentley George s George, Holborn, lapidary to John Chupsey 12 Apr 1781
Berkeley Robert s Robert, citizen and merchant tailor to his father 9 Apr 1718
Berkley Rowland s Maurice, Apethorpe, Nth, gentleman to John Berkley, citizen and haberdasher 19 Apr 1699
Berriman John s John, citizen and apothecary† to John Burrows 12 Jul 1706
Berry William s William, Turnbell Street, baker to Hewson Scott 14 Oct 1736
Best Richard s Robert to John Jones 12 Dec 1754
Betteridge John s Thomas, Charterhouse Lane, Mdx, ostler to William Gascoyne 16 Aug 1722
Bettsworth William s Jacob, Southwark, Sry to William Barnes, citizen and weaver 17 Aug 1714
Bibbin Thomas s John to Daniel Butler 10 Apr 1755
Bickley Samuel s Samuel to Mary Burrell 8 mar 1764
Biddle Isaac s James, citizen and scrivener to John Smith, citizen and weaver 31 Mar 1703
Bingham Thomas s Richard† to John Studdard 9 Oct 1760
Bird John s John, Worcester, Wor, yeoman† to Samuel Morris 23 Mar 1704/5 <6 May 1709 turned over to George Sewell; free>
Bird Sarah d Thomas, Epsom, Sry, coachman to William Bird 25 Jul 1723
Bird Thomas s Thomas, Epsom, Sry, coachman to Thomas Pensom, citizen and haberdasher 31 Aug 1698 <free>
Bird William s Richard, Epsom, Sry to William Gutteridge, citizen and longbowstringmaker 20 Jul 1714 <free>
Birkhead Wilson s Robert, citizen and armourer to Elizabeth Harris 14 Mar 1722/3 <free>
Blackford John s Daniel to Catherine How 9 Sep 1756
Bladon William s Samuel, Cow Cross, Mdx, yeoman to Robert Reynolds 18 Sep 1810
Blake Bridget d Richard, Overton, Ham, yeoman to Richard Blake 10 Sep 1712
Blakesly William s John, St Botolph Aldersgate, tailor to John Burton 13 Jul 1732
Blakeston John s Mary to James White 10 Sep 1741
Blanch James s Thomas, St Margaret Westminster, Mdx to his father 11 Feb 1779
Blanch Thomas s John, Clerkenwell, Mdx, labourer to William Gascoyne 26 Apr 1739
Blanch Thomas s Thomas to his father 12 Apr 1770
Blancowe Christopher Clarke s John, Stony Stratford, Bkm, joiner to Joseph Tucker 19 Aug 1702 <free>
Blankinsopp Thomas s Thomas, Blankinsopp Castle, Nbl, esq. to Christopher Blower, citizen and haberdasher 9 Nov 1694 <dead>
Bluet John s John, citizen and haberdasher† to John Finch 6 Mar 1715/6
Booker Samuel s James, Old Street, weaver† to Luke Sympson 13 Oct 1737
Booth Thomas s Thomas, St Martin in the Fields, Mdx, tailor to Charles Scott 26 May 1790
Booth William Fryer s William, St Martin in the Fields, Mdx, stablekeeper to Francis Cabell 14 Apr 1726 <26 Aug 1729 discharged for non-enrollment; 30 Dec 1730 to Francis again>
Bound Richard s Richard, Huggin Lane, Lnd† to George Wohlman 19 Nov 1801
Bourke William s John, Chapel Street, Bedford Row, Mdx, chocolate maker† to James Crooke 12 Jul 1733
Bourne John s Ebenezer, St James Clerkenwell, whitesmith to Edward Davis (widow) 10 Jun 1736
Bowden Joseph s Richard, Bristol, Gls† to John Waller 12 Dec 1745
Bowry George Crew s Thomas, Iver, Bkm, carpenter to Henry Deeves 14 Dec 1807
Boyce Thomas s Thomas to Daniel Butler 8 Feb 1759
Boyle Benjamin s Benjamin to Samuel Roberts 9 Sep 1779 <10 Jun 1784 turned over to Benjamin Roberts>
Boys Nicholas s Thomas to George Naylor 12 Mar 1767
Boys Thomas s Thomas to his father 8 Mar 1787
Bradford Charles s Samuel to John Strong 11 Jun 1761
Bradford Francis s Joseph, Dunstable, Bdf, glazier to James Douglas, citizen and merchant tailor 28 Jul 1709 <free>
Bradford Samuel s Samuel to John Macey 14 Jul 1757
Bradley Benjamin s Benjamin, Golden Lane, Mdx, tailor to Joseph Johnson 19 Jun 1809
Bradshaw John s Richard, Aldersgate Street, labourer late† to Joseph Tucker 13 Mar 1728/9
Bradshaw William s William, Deene, Nth, apothecary† to William Williams, citizen and merchant tailor 18 Sep 1706 <dead>

GOLD AND SILVER WYRE DRAWERS' APPRENTICESHIPS

Brady John s John, Shoreditch, Mdx, watch chainmaker to Thomas Cowald 12 Jul 1781
Brandon Charles s John† to Francis Wilkinson 12 Oct 1749
Branfield John s Stephen, Mdx, glover† to John Hughes, citizen and goldsmith 26 Jul 1704 <free>
Bressey Richard Burr s William, Spitalfields, Mdx, cooper to Peter Duke 16 Dec 1814
Bridge Thomas Timothy s George, St Giles Cripplegate, toymaker to William McDonald 3 Nov 1829
Bristow Robert s Timothy, citizen and brewer† to Thomas Bishop 28 Jul 1698 <free>
Brittain John s John, Silver Street, Wood Street, wiredrawer† to Richard Panton, citizen and clothworker 9 Dec 1725
Broad Robert s Francis to William Stackhouse 13 Mar 1760
Brock John s John, Bermondsey, Sry, leatherdresser to John Winter 8 Jun 1721 <dead>
Bromfield James s James, St Mary Overy, wheelwright to Walter Crew (jnr.) 8 Jan 1707/8
Brookes John s Jonathan to James Dennis 8 Jul 1756 (charity of St Lawrence Reading, Brk)
Brooks Richard s Jonathan to James Dennis 11 Dec 1760 (charity of St Lawrence Reading, Brk)
Brooksby Villeors s Edward, Lnd, vintner to Edward Brooksby, citizen and blacksmith 26 Nov 1717
Broome James s Stephen, Bicester, Oxf, fellmonger to Robert Glyde 12 Nov 1719
Broome Joseph s Stephen, Bicester, Oxf, fellmonger to John Dodsworth 2 Oct 1716 <free>
Brown Henry s John, Leominster, Hef, butcher to John Blackwell, cit. & blacksmith 14 Nov 1709
Brown John s Simon, St Luke, Mdx, labourer to John Miles 14 Feb 1771
Brown Joseph s John, St Giles Cripplegate, Mdx, turner to Thomas Winston 24 Apr 1696 <free>
Brown Thomas s Thomas to George Naylor 9 Sep 1779 <14 Sep 1780 turned over to John Richardson>
Brown William s Philip† to John Richardson 13 Sep 1787
Brown William s William, mariner† to Sarah Cabell (widow) 14 Mar 1744/5
Bryan Henry s Henry to Richard Burch 10 Oct 1765
Bryan Samuel s Samuel to Samuel Roberts 14 Jul 1768
Bryant Benjamin s Edmund, citizen and wax chandler to Edward Langden, citizen and cordwainer 5 Sep 1706
Buckland Samuel s Samuel to William Stackhouse 11 Mar 1762
Budworth Charles William s William, Chelsea, Mdx† to John Read 11 Oct 1781
Bull William s Henry, citizen and haberdasher† to Ralph Dormer 14 Apr 1720 <free>
Bullmore William s Richard, Hamble, Ham, mariner to James Scovell 17 Jan 1820 <free>
Burch Edward s Thomas to Henry Questead 11 Sep 1755
Burch Richard s William to John Jones 14 Oct 1756
Burch William s William to Joseph Bowden 11 Mar 1762
Burgin John s Thomas to his father 15 Oct 1804
Burgin John s John, Thames Street, Lnd to his father 27 Sep 1827
Burgin Thomas s Thomas to his father 14 Mar 1799
Burgin Thomas s Thomas to his father 9 May 1832
Burgis Thomas s James to John Green 14 Jul 1768 (charity of Cheshunt, Hrt) <13 Feb 1772 turned over to John Turner>
Burgis William s William, Godstone, Sry, yeoman to Joseph Tucker 24 Jul 1697 <free>
Burgisse Robert s Robert, Urchfont, Wil, yeoman to Edward Langdell, citizen and cordwainer 4 Sep 1718
Burne Richard s Joseph, Lambeth, Sry, gentleman to John Ashmead 4 Jun & 8 Jun 1728
Burnett George s George† to William Read 10 Apr 1755
Burnett James s Jane, Nightingale Lane, widow to John Winter 10 Nov 1726 <free>
[*last entry unnotated* 'F']
Burnett Robert s John to George Townsend 14 May 1767
Burrell Abraham s Abraham, Wapping, Mdx, shipwright to David Taylor 10 Aug 1732
Burrell John s William to William Turner 9 Nov 1758
Burrell William s John, Swan Alley, victualler to William Bull 14 Oct 1736 <8 Apr 1742 turned over to (Mrs) Gascoyne>
Burridge John s William, St Giles Cripplegate to Thomas Wagstaffe, citizen and merchant tailor 26 Apr 1708
Burroughs John Thomas s John to Charles Bull 11 May 1769
Burrutt Clement s Nicholas, Kentish Town, Mdx, labourer to Robert Neall 4 Feb 1717/8 <free>
Burton James s James to John Proudley 29 Nov 1787

GOLD AND SILVER WYRE DRAWERS' APPRENTICESHIPS

Burton John s Thomas, Dublin† to Thomas Pensom, citizen and haberdasher 13 Jul 1694 <free>
Busher John s John, citizen and carpenter to Marmaduke Isles 11 Apr 1745
Bushnell Henry s John, Crutched Friars, Lnd, bricklayer to Samuel Marshall 14 Mar 1733/4
Butcher John s John, St Sepulchre, Lnd, yeoman to William Sansum 14 Mar 1799
Butler Daniel s Daniel, citizen and blacksmith to Goodwin Washbourne 3 Jan 1715/6 <free>
Butler Robert s John, St Lawrence Reading, Brk, tailor to George Martin 14 May 1778
Buxton Charles s Thomas to Daniel How 11 Sep 1746
Buxton Robert s Robert, 'Graunton', Sfk, sergemaker to John Joseph 3 Jul 1701

Cabell Francis s Francis, Cosgrove, Nth, labourer to Joseph Tucker 9 Jan 1704/5 <free>
Camfield William s William, Whetstone, Mdx, yeoman to Thomas Brock,
   citizen and merchant tailor 18 Jun 1713 <free>
Camroux Ferdinand Ferguson s Ferdinand Richard, Bucklersbury, Lnd to his father 27 Jan 1826
Camroux Ferdinand Richard s John Lewis, citizen and gold and silver wyre drawer to
   Ferdinand de Medina 16 May 1804
Camroux John Lewis s John Simon to Thomas Collins 10 Nov 1763
Carpender Stephen s Stephen, St Bartholomew the Less, Lnd, apothecary to Richard Blake
   3 Jun 1697 <free>
Carr Edward s Edward, citizen and clothworker† to Thomas Gardiner, citizen and fishmonger
   10 Nov 1699 <free>
Carr George Panton s George Lewis to Joseph Brown 9 Feb 1769 <13 Apr 1775 turned over to
   Thomas Currier>
Carter George s William, White Cross Street, tailor to Edward Edwards 11 Nov 1736
※Carter Joseph s Robert, citizen & blacksmith† to Thomas Gardiner, cit. & fishmonger 19 Jan 1698/9
※Carter Joseph s Joseph to Solomon Harris 10 Oct 1751
Carter Richard s George to Thomas White 8 Jul 1762
Cartwright Robert s Robert to John Mayor 12 Mar 1789
Cauvin Michael s James, St Martin in the Fields, Mdx, gentleman to Thomas Wells,
   citizen and longbowstringmaker 22 Dec 1709
Cavell Thomas s Henry to William Corneck Martin 14 Jun 1764
Chalmers John s John to John Edwards 8 Oct 1767 <14 Mar 1771 turned over to
   Thomas Chapman>
Chalmers Thomas s William, St Saviour Southwark, Sry, smith to John Chalmers 16 Jul 1801
Chamberlayne Joseph s Mathew, Much Cowarne, Hef, clerk to (Mr) Prosser,
   citizen and merchant tailor 28 Jun 1711
Chambers Robert s Robert to Charles Bull 10 Jun 1762
Champion Joshua s Joshua, Sulham Bannister, Bkm, grocer to Richard Burch 13 Jun 1776
Chandler Percival s Thomas to his father 9 May 1723 <free>
Chandler Thomas s Thomas, Soulbury, Bkm, yeoman to John Gardner, citizen and goldsmith
   2 Feb 1698/9 <free>
Chapman Robert s Jane, widow to James White 8 Nov 1744
Chapman Thomas s Thomas to John Green 13 Dec 1750
Chapman Thomas s Thomas to his father 5 Jul 1796
Chapman William s Jonathan, Woodford, Nth, saddler to Thomas Wagstaffe 31 Jul 1714
Charlesworth James s William to William Turner 12 Feb 1761
Cheshire William s William, Cheshunt, Hrt, yeoman to John Burrows 1 Apr 1708 <turned over to
   Thomas Brock for want of enrolling; this indenture served out 15 Dec 1714>
Chew-Porter Elisha s Elisha, St Dunstan in the West, Lnd. vintner† to Martin Catling,
   citizen and cordwainer 19 Jun 1701
Child John s John, Shoreditch, Mdx, weaver to William Shaw 12 Feb 1735/6 <10 Aug 1738
   turned over to (Mr) Munt>
Chupsey John s John† to Solomon Harris 12 Jan 1758
Churchman John s William to Benjamin Roberts 7 Sep 1789
Churchman John s William† to John Churchman (snr.) 3 Sep 1817
Churchman William s William† to Edward Dennis 29 Nov 1787 <13 Aug 1794 turned over to
   Thomas Cowald>
Churchman William s William late gold and silver wyre drawer to John Churchman 19 Sep 1809
Clark James s John to Henry Questead 12 Apr 1764 <13 Feb 1772 turned over to Mary Edwards>

GOLD AND SILVER WYRE DRAWERS' APPRENTICESHIPS

Clark John s James† to Thomas Marriott 12 Feb 1746/7
Clark William s John, Hagborne, Brk, yeoman to John Martin, cit. & merchant tailor 21 Mar 1703/4
Clarke Daniel s Thomas, Norton Folgate, Mdx, mathematical instrument maker to Samuel Crouch 8 Jul 1731
Clarkson Thomas s John, Stepney, Mdx, calico printer to Mathew Price 28 Feb 1714/5
Clay John s Thomas, citizen & weaver† to Peter Archer, cit. & haberdasher 8 May 1704 <free>
Clay Joseph s Joseph, Coggeshall, Ess, gentleman to William Gutteridge, citizen and longbowstringmaker 1 Jul 1698 <free>
Clements John s Thomas, Waddenham, Bkm, labourer to William Burgesse 13 Jun 1707 <6 May 1709 turned over to William Ganton, citizen and goldsmith>
Clerke James s James, Wooler, Nbl, yeoman to Joseph Tucker, cit. & merchant tailor 30 Mar 1694
Clifford William s James, Glasshouse Yard, St Botolph Aldersgate, glass cutter to Joseph Johnson 10 Jul 1820
Clotworthy Benjamin s Leonard, St Giles Cripplegate, Mdx, weaver† to John Day, citizen and cordwainer 10 Aug 1694 <dead>
Clouet Christopher s Ann, widow to Francis Houlton 14 Jun 1744
Coates John s John, Mdx, shoemaker to Wandell Winter, citizen and blacksmith 26 Jun 1702
Coker Robert s Thomas† to James Fowler 12 Mar 1746/7
Colcomb William s John, Queenhithe, Lnd, waterman to John May 25 Jun 1818
Cold William s Edmund, White Cross Street to Richard Littlewood 10 Sep 1724 <17 May 1727 turned over by Richard's execs. to John Walter>
Cole Henry s Thomas, Grantham, Lin, gentleman to Samuel Pharrow, citizen and vintner 13 Jul 1694 <dead>
Coleman William s Stephen, Jewin Street, cabinet maker to Thomas Prosser, citizen and merchant tailor 10 May 1733
Collard Stephen s Ann, Moor Lane, Lnd, widow to Edward Finch 14 Feb 1722/3
Collett Edward s William† to Joseph Carter 9 Apr 1761
Collett John s John, Stow, Gls to Thomas Shovell 13 Jun 1745
Collier Richard s Henry, Basingstoke, Ham, shoemaker to James Booth, citizen and blacksmith 30 Nov 1697 <free>
Collins Daniel s William† to Philip Collins 13 Feb 1745/6
Collins Thomas s Philip to his father 14 Aug 1740
Collins Thomas s Peter to David Taylor 11 Feb 1747/8
Collins Thomas s Thomas† to John Green 13 May 1756
Collis Edward s Thomas, Lnd, goldsmith† to John Watkin 29 Jan 1717/8
Combebrune Michael s Peter, Soho, Mdx, esquire† to Daniel Mallory 12 Oct 1732
Cook Henry s John to Joseph Gregory 8 Jul 1762
Cook John Hamond s Stephen, Rotherhithe, Sry, staymaker to John Whinnell 10 Jun 1725 <free>
Cook Samuel s John, citizen and goldsmith to Charles Hosier, citizen and goldsmith 23 Mar 1705/6
Cook William s Augustine, South Audley Street, Mdx, tea factor to Noah Roberts 13 Oct 1795
Cooke Philip s Richard, St Giles in the Fields, Mdx, shoemaker to Elizabeth Davis (widow) 8 Aug 1734 <10 Jul 1735 turned over to Edward Nott>
Cooke Richard s Richard, Islington, Mdx, merchant† to James Grammer, citizen and goldsmith 26 Jun 1717 <free>
Cooke Timothy s John, Shrewsbury, Sal, draper to John Cooke, citizen and goldsmith 14 Mar 1699/1700 <free>
Cooper John s John, Bromley St Leonard, Mdx, apothecary to Francis Wootton, citizen and haberdasher 8 Jul 1731
Corbett Richard s Waties, St Martin in the Fields, Mdx, gentleman to James ... 24 Mar 1697/8
Corral Christopher s Christopher to John Pope 14 Aug 1746
Correy James s James to Thomas Shovel 14 Aug 1746
Costa Abraham Gomes Da s Moses Gomes to Moses Hart 27 Feb 1834
Cotton Benjamin s Elisha, Grub Street, Lnd, surgeon to Robert Glyde 13 Dec 1722 <free>
Cotton John Pole s Benjamin to Samuel Roberts 9 Jul 1747
Cotton William s Benjamin to his father 10 Jan 1750/1
Court John s Benjamin, Warwick, War, wheelwright to John Lane, citizen and weaver 31 Jan 1706/7 <free>
Courtney Edward s William to Richard Wrathall turned over to Mary Read 11 Feb 1768

GOLD AND SILVER WYRE DRAWERS' APPRENTICESHIPS

Courtney Richard s William, Shoreditch, Mdx, perukemaker to John Scarnell 9 Apr 1772
Couzens John s John, White Cross Street, weaver to John Winter 12 Jan 1737/8
Cowcher Thomas s Thomas, Southwark, Sry, vintner† to Pauncefoot Greene 1 Mar 1705/6
Coweld Christopher s Daniel, Spitalfields, Mdx to John Winter 14 Dec 1732
Cowley Claudius s John, Brewer Street, St James Westminster, Mdx† to John Walklate 8 May 1735
    [*in margin* 'Whinnell']
Cowley Samuel s Roger, citizen and turner† to Peter Moore, citizen and blacksmith 6 Dec 1703
Cowley William s William, Lnd, tailor to Henry Barton, citizen and grocer 8 Jun 1714 <free>
Cox Charles s James, Bloomsbury, Mdx, coachman to James Millist 28 Oct 1833
Cox Robert s Robert† to Daniel How 14 Jun 1750
Crafts Edward s William, Chick Lane, Lnd, labourer to Robert Neal 8 Oct 1730
Crane John Sermon s John Sermon† to Robert Wrathall 4 Jun 1750
Crew Walter s Mathew, Wotton under Edge, Gls, clothworker to John Shaler,
    citizen and merchant tailor 16 Aug 1693 <free>
Crook James s Francis, citizen and cordwainer to Thomas Prosser, citizen and merchant tailor
    8 Jul 1713 <free>
Crookshanks John s John, Stratford Langthorne, Ess, barber to Joseph Tucker 30 Mar 1738
Cropley St.John Harton s Samuel to Daniel How 8 Oct 1761
Crouch Samuel s Thomas, citizen & plasterer to Thomas Winston, cit. & clothworker 23 Apr 1703
Crouch Stephen s Samuel to his father 11 Apr 1734
Crow John s Robert to Thomas Alstone 10 Jul 1746
Cruse Jeremiah s Archelaus, Little Britain, Lnd, yeoman to Joseph Johnson 18 Nov 1803
Cruttenden Daniel s Thomas, citizen and cooper to William Banks 11 Oct 1744
Cubbidge James s George, Bow, Mdx, yeoman to John Proudley .. Jul 1792
Cunliff Nicholas s Nicholas, Accrington, Lan, gentleman to Robert Berkley,
    citizen and merchant tailor 9 Nov 1694 <free>
Cunliffe Nicholas s Nicholas to his father 9 May 1723 <free>
Cunliffe William Madgwick s Nicholas, Lnd to Richard Cluer 8 Oct 1724 <14 May 1730 turned
    over to his father; free>
Currie William s William, Holborn, Mdx, bedsteadmaker to George Edenbury 7 Dec 1809
Curryer Thomas s William, citizen and wheelwright† to William Turner 8 Aug 1745
Curtis Thomas s Richard, New Street, Lnd to Edward Mottrom 13 Apr 1780

Da Costa *see* Costa
Dadford Richard s Jonathan to Thomas Chapman 18 May 1788
Dale Robert s George, St Botolph Aldersgate, innholder to John Read 11 Apr 1771
Darby Robert s John, St Andrew Undershaft, Lnd, carver and gilder to Samuel Read 13 Jun 1782
Dark Thomas s Thomas, Whitechapel, Mdx, gunsmith† to John Dodsworth 10 Jun 1725 <free>
Darke Daniel s Richard to John Aylesbury 8 Oct 1767
Davill Robert s Joshua, citizen and packer to Arabella Field, widow 15 Sep 1708 <free>
Davis Edward s John, Llanmerewig, Mgy, yeoman† to George Turberville 16 Oct 1707 <free>
Davis Edward s Edward, Fore Street, Lnd† to William Hewes 20 Mar 1732/3
Davis Edward s Jeremiah, citizen and weaver† to Sarah Cabell (widow) 10 May 1744
Davis Edward s Edward to Edward Davis 14 May 1761
Davis George s Charles to Mary Sweeting 14 Jul 1748
Davis George s Sidaway to William Sansum 4 Jun 1804
Davis James s Zachariah, Old Street, mariner† to Richard Smelt 14 Dec 1732
Davis James s Joseph, Philip Lane, London Wall, Lnd to Samuel Fenton Read 21 Jun 1823
    <9 Jul 1825 turned over to John Barnes, citizen and loriner>
Davis John s John† to James Laxton 10 Nov 1757
Davis John s Richard to Christopher Cowald 12 May 1763
Davis Philip s Thomas to Elizabeth Gascoyne 11 Dec 1746
Davis Samuel s Timothy to Thomas Blanch 13 May 1756
Davis Silvanus s Edward, citizen and weaver to Mark Baily 12 Sep 1743
Davison Joshua s John, Fleet Street, Lnd, laceman to Francis Wootton, citizen and haberdasher
    14 Sep 1738
Davy Godfrey s Edward, citizen and merchant tailor† to James Douglas, citizen and vintner
    4 Feb 1717/8 <sued out of his indentures>

GOLD AND SILVER WYRE DRAWERS' APPRENTICESHIPS

Dawkins Frederick s William, Benjamin Street, Cow Cross to Thomas Etherington 7 Nov 1826
Dawkins John s John, Newington, Sry, carpenter to John Green 10 Jun 1736
Dawkins Nathaniel s John, Spitalfields, Mdx, wiredrawer to Daniel Fisher 14 Feb 1722/3
Dawkins Samuel s John, Guildford, Sry† to John Green 12 Mar 1740/1
Dawson John s John, Lambeth, Sry† to John Chapman 24 Jul 1815
Dawson Robert s Robert, labourer to John Underwood 13 Dec 1744
Day John s Henry, Southwark, Sry, labourer to Benjamin Russle, citizen and weaver 4 May 1714
Dayles John s William, Newington Green, Sry to Benjamin Goff 13 Jun 1734
Dayles William s William† to John Dayles 11 Jun 1747
Dayling Richard s Richard, East Smithfield, gentleman to Francis Cabell 9 Jun 1737
Deane James s Ann, widow to Percival Chandler 12 Jul 1744
Deeves Henry s Samuel, Little Britain, Lnd, victualler† to John Read 11 Sep 1794
De Medina Ferdinand s Solomon, Stoke Newington, gentleman to John Lewis Camroux 8 Apr 1790
Dennis Edward s Thomas to Thomas Dennis 13 Oct 1748
Dennis James s Edward, Wycombe, Bkm, yeoman to John Walklate 12 Jun 1735
Dennis William s Thomas† to John Scarnell 14 Dec 1769 <12 Sep 1771 turned over to James Dennis>
Devon Samuel s Samuel to Daniel How 9 Jun 1743
Dewin Benjamin s Thomas, St Botolph Aldersgate† to John Walklate 10 Nov 1743
Dewin Benjamin s Benjamin to William Turner 11 Mar 1779
Dewin Thomas s Thomas† to Elizabeth Harris 11 Aug 1743
Diggory Samuel s Samuel, Lnd, labourer to Francis Wotton, citizen and haberdasher 12 May 1720 <30 Aug 1722 turned over to Robert Crew; free>
Dingley Edward s Edward, Bridgewater Square, Barbican to Edward Stilwell 1 Aug 1828
Diss Moses s Richard, Grub Street, Lnd, yeoman to George Truscoat 28 Mar 1814
Dixon Henry s John to George Naylor 14 Jul 1763
Dodd James s James, Gloucester, Gls, yeoman† to Walter Turner 19 Aug 1703 <free>
Dormar James s Francis, citizen and founder† to Ralph Dormar 7 Jun 1705 <free>
Doughty Michael s Michael, victualler to William Read 14 Oct 1742
Douglas George s George, Hendon, Mdx† to John Haynes 10 Feb 1736/7 <12 Apr 1739 turned over to Robert Wrathall>
Dowdall Starling s Gabriel, citizen and weaver to George Meakins, citizen 27 Apr 1699 <free>
Downer Joseph s Joseph, Wild Street, Mdx, tailor† to James William Hearne 16 Nov 1814
Dowson William s William† to Thomas Simpson 8 Oct 1761
Drabwell William s Richard to Joseph Atkinson 9 Jan 1766
Drake John s Lawrence, Gretton, Nth to Edward Turner, citizen and longbowstringmaker 15 Aug 1706 <free>
Draper John s Joseph to Stephen Crouch 14 Dec 1752
Draycott William s William, Old St., labourer to Orme Quarry, citizen and cordwainer 11 May 1727
Ducker Michael s George, St James Clerkenwell, Mdx to George Newport, citizen and coachmaker 10 Oct 1782
Duffield John s John, Lydney, Gls, yeoman† to James Douglas, cit. & vintner 3 Nov 1714 <free>
Duffield Peter s Peter, Chelsea, Mdx, pensioner to James Reynolds 27 Jan 1820 <free>
Duke Peter s Peter to Richard Sturley 11 May 1769
Duncomb Cowen s John, Bell Alley, Cripplegate, carpenter to John Burton 8 Jul 1725
Dunkley Robert s Thomas, Great ..., Lei to Joseph Tucker 3 Mar 1712/3 <free>
Dunnill James s Francis to John Gifford 13 Feb 1745/6
Durbridge George s John, Halford, War, cordwainer† to John Owen, citizen and longbowstringmaker 12 Nov 1705
Duson Joseph s Joseph, Mdx, labourer to Thomas Bracy, citizen and grocer 30 Jun 1703
Dyde Philip s John, St Luke, Mdx, leatherdresser to Thomas Pitcher 8 Oct 1778

Eades Thomas s Thomas, Birmingham, War, cutler to James Douglas, one of this company, citizen and vintner 12 Sep 1728
Eagle William s John, St James Clerkenwell, Mdx, glass scalloper to Henry Riviers 13 Nov 1729
Eamonson Joshua s Joshua, Grays Inn, Mdx, gentleman to Thomas Birch 10 Feb 1780
Eden Thomas s Mathew, Old Street, vintner to William Read 10 Feb 1736/7
Edenbury John s John to Thomas Blanch 12 Mar 1761

GOLD AND SILVER WYRE DRAWERS' APPRENTICESHIPS

Ederingaine Thomas s John, citizen and fletcher† to John Stanton 5 Aug 1700 <free>
Ederingham Thomas s Thomas to his father 11 Aug 1726
Edgecomb Ogle Arthur s George, near Exeter, Dev, gentleman to James Douglas 13 Jul 1721
Edsaw John s Thomas to Robert Saunders 8 Sep 1768 <11 Apr 1771 turned over to
    John Chupsey>
Edwards Edward nephew of John Lewis, White Cross Street, Lnd, husbandman to Joseph Everett
    10 Jan 1722/3 <free - dead>
Edwards John s Jane, widow to Mark Baily 9 Dec 1742
Edwards Thomas s Edward† to Henry Questeard 9 Jan 1752
Edwin Edmund s William, Carrington, [no county given] ?Chs or Lin, yeoman to John Ferris
    13 Jul 1738 <15 Jul 1740 turned over to Andrew Aylesbury>
Elderton Maund s Edward, Stratford on Avon, War, innholder to James Parratt 23 Dec 1697
Elgar Thomas s Francis to Mary Simpson 9 Oct 1746
Eliot John s Jeremy, East Markham, Ntt, yeoman to John Shaler, citizen and merchant tailor
    12 Oct 1694 <dead>
Elkin James s John† to Robert Crew 12 Mar 1746/7
Elliot Thomas s Walter, Wicken, Cam, maltster† to John Ferris 8 Jun 1732
Elliott George s George, Shipton [? Slapton], Bkm, yeoman to Edmund Sollers,
    citizen and merchant tailor 1 Apr 1697 <dead>
Elliott Stephen s Philip to James Laxton 9 Apr 1761
Ellis John s John, St Giles Cripplegate, Mdx, needlemaker† to William Gutteridge,
    citizen and longbowstringmaker 1 May 1705
Emblyn John s John, citizen and grocer† to Robert Neale 17 Sep 1707
Embry John s William, citizen and glover† to George Sewell 30 Dec 1707 <2 Jul 1713 turned over
    to ... Webb, citizen and longbowstringmaker; free>
Essex Benjamin s Dennis, Stretton, War, labourer† to William Cartwright 11 Sep 1707
Etherington Thomas s George, Fetter Lane, greengrocer to Joseph Johnson 8 Feb 1814
Evans James s Robert, White Cross Street, yeoman to Robert Evans (jnr.) 15 Jun 1803
Evans John s Stephen, Jewin Street, Lnd, brandy seller† to John Green 8 Jun 1732
Evans John s John to his father 13 Oct 1763
Evans John s William to his father 11 Oct 1770
Evans Robert s Robert, White Cross Street, Lnd, victualler to Edward Hales 12 Jun 1794
Evans William s John, Petticoat Lane, yeoman to Henry Riviers 30 Mar 1737 <9 Oct 1740
    turned over to (Mr) Aylesbury>
Evatt Joseph s Joseph, Taunton, Som, linen draper to Joseph Carter 13 Aug 1778

Fairbrother John s Thomas, citizen and salter to William Cowley 14 Nov 1723 <free>
Falmer Richard s John, Lnd, ironmonger to John Dodsworth 26 Oct 1714
Fancourt Richard s Lyon, Glaston, Rut, gentleman to Joseph Chamberlaine, citizen and grocer
    20 Nov 1698
Farmer John s John, citizen & ironmonger to Thomas Brock, citizen & merchant tailor 19 Sep 1705
Farr John s George, Apsley, Bdf, yeoman to Mark Bailey 10 Jul 1735
Farr Mark s John to Sarah Burnett 10 Jun 1762
Farr William s George, Bdf, yeoman to Thomas Alston 11 Oct 1744
Faulkner Thomas s Thomas, Shoreditch, Mdx, weaver† to Richard Drury 9 Sep 1731
Faveryear Thomas s Samuel, citizen and coachmaker to John Walklate 12 Sep 1745
Fearn Joseph s Samuel to his father 12 Mar 1789
Fearn Samuel s Hugh† to John Salmon 14 Mar 1765
Fell George s Francis, Grub Street, buttonhole turner to his father 11 Feb 1724/5
Ferne Walter s George, Lambeth, Sry, sweep to William Read 9 Aug 1739
Ferris John s Elias, Malmesbury, Wil, gentleman to William Gutteridge,
    citizen and longbowstringmaker 23 Aug 1693 <free>
Fielding James s James, St James Westminster, Mdx, glazier to John Embry 11 May 1721
Figgitt Benjamin s Benjamin, Holywell Mount, Mdx, yeoman† to Robert Reynolds 2 Jul 1804
Fillison James s Thomas† to Samuel Roberts 8 Jul 1762
Fillison Thomas s James to Thomas Chapman 23 Jul 1789
Fillon William s John, Spitalfields, Mdx, weaver to Charles Scott 26 Oct 1784

GOLD AND SILVER WYRE DRAWERS' APPRENTICESHIPS

Finch John s Robert, St Giles Cripplegate, Mdx, weaver to George Butter, citizen and stationer 18 Aug 1704 <free>
Finch Joseph s Edward, Lnd, weaver to Richard Tuthill 9 Sep 1717 <19 Jan 1720/1 turned over to Thomas Sharpe>
Fisher George s Robert, Lnd, dyer† to John Cordrey, citizen and shipwright 19 Jun 1717
Flammire Charles s John, Shoreditch, Mdx, weaver to John Churchman 13 Jun 1809
Fleming George s George, Bermondsey, Sry, waterman to James William Hearne 30 Mar 1833
Forward Jonathan s James, Stoke, Som, yeoman to John Gardner, cit. & goldsmith 13 Mar 1703/4
Fosnold George s Charles, Pimlico, Mdx to Stephen Crouch 9 Sep 1833
Fowler Hugh s Rees, Pem to John Waller 13 Dec 1744
Fowler James s ... to Robert Crew 10 Jun 1736
Fowler James s James to his father 9 Nov 1758
Fowler John s Jonathan, St Giles Cripplegate, Lnd to his father 9 Mar 1775
Fowler Jonathan s Jonathan, Wapping, Mdx, silk dyer to Robert Crew 10 Jan 1739/40
Francis Samuel s John, citizen and pewterer† to Daniel Collins, citizen and girdler 3 Mar 1698/9
Franklin John s Berton, Botolph Claydon, Bkm, grazier to John Green, citizen and goldsmith 16 Aug 1693
Franklin William s William, Shrewsbury, Sal, yeoman to Joshua Eamonson 28 Mar 1801
Franklyn Thomas s Thomas, Aldersgate Street† to Nicholas Cunliffe 14 Aug 1735
Franklyn William s William, Grub Street, Cripplegate, gilder† to Thomas Chandler 8 Jul 1725 <23 Mar 1725/6 turned over by Eleanor Chandler (widow) to James Worsley>
Frazier John s Thomas to Stephen Goome 9 Apr 1761
Freeman Mathew s James, Bermondsey, Sry, cheesemonger† to James Norton 9 Nov 1792
Freeman Thomas s John to Samuel Roberts 10 Aug 1769
French James s Joseph, Stepney, Mdx to John Taylor 27 Jun 1822
French John s Robert, Groton, Sfk to George French 5 Jun 1716 <31 May 1722 turned over to John Frouchon>
French Richard s John, Theydon Bois, Ess, yeoman† to John Ford, citizen and cordwainer 28 Mar 1698 <free>
French Samuel s John† to John Underwood 13 Sep 1753
Fry George s Richard, Barton, Som, baker to John Hills, citizen and goldsmith 12 Sep 1718
Frye George s Richard, Charlton Adam, Som, baker to John Whinnell 10 Apr 1716
Fryer John s William to John Jones 8 Oct 1767
Fuller Mathew s Joseph, Woolwich, Ken, yeoman to Peter Duke 3 Aug 1801

Gandy James s James, Limehouse, Mdx, mariner to John Turner 26 Aug 1800
Gardener Thomas s Thomas, Painswick, Gls, clothworker to James Douglas, citizen and fishmonger 10 Jul 1699 <free>
Gardner Daniel s Daniel, Wotton under Edge, Gls to Robert Crew 14 Dec 1732
Gardner John s John, St Martin in the Fields, Mdx, tailor to John Wainwright 12 May 1719
Gardner Thomas s Thomas, High Holborn, Mdx, tallow chandler to Richard Pugh 6 Oct 1804
Garfield William s ... to Henry Sparrow 12 Sep 1827
Garret Thomas s William, Long Alley, weaver to John Hills, citizen and goldsmith 14 Mar 1727/8
Gascoign Robert s Robert, citizen and blacksmith to Oliver Richmond 21 Mar 1699/1700 <free>
George Richard Henry s Richard, Tyler Street, Mdx, fishmonger to John Richardson 14 Nov 1796
Gerrard James s James, St Martin in the Fields, Mdx, cordwainer to John Whinnell 9 Jun 1719 <gone away five years>
Gibbons Thomas s John, Bermondsey, Sry† to Richard Bird, citizen and blacksmith 9 Nov 1698
Gilberthorpe Robert s Richard, Whittington, Dby, yeoman to John Cumberlidge 26 Sep 1712
Glide Robert s Stephen, Broxted, Ess, yeoman to Benjamin Negus, citizen and merchant tailor 7 Mar 1704/5 <free>
Godwin Thomas s Joseph, Wookey, Som, gentleman to Thomas Wagstaff, citizen and merchant tailor 19 Jan 1699/1700 <free>
Goffe Benjamin s William, Edwardstone, Sfk, clerk† to Benjamin Negus, citizen and merchant tailor 31 Jul 1718
Goldsmith Dennis s Mathew, citizen and silk throster† to Thomas Godwyn 6 Nov 1716
Goldsworthy Thomas s William, Commercial Road, Mdx, ropemaker to John Taylor 26 Oct 1813
Goldsworthy William s William, Commercial Road, Mdx, ropemaker to John Taylor 16 Feb 1813

GOLD AND SILVER WYRE DRAWERS' APPRENTICESHIPS

Gomes Da Costa *see* Costa
Gomm John s William to John Beer 9 Aug 1781
Gomm William s John, White Cross Street, Mdx† to John Beer 13 Dec 1804
Goodacre Thomas s John, Hackney, Mdx, carpenter to Richard Birch 23 Mar 1801
Goodman John s Andrew, Edmonton, Mdx, yeoman to (Mr) Wrathall 12 May 1737
Goodyear Nathaniel s William to Samuel Roberts 10 Aug 1758
Goold James s John, Clerkenwell, Mdx, yeoman to James Scovell 22 Apr 1812
Goome Stephen to John Winter 11 Jun 1741 <8 Aug 1745 turned over to John Maccartney>
Gootheridge Joseph s Joseph† to Joseph Allen turned over to Samuel Roberts 8 Nov 1770
Gostick John s William, White Cross Street, Mdx, yeoman to John Turner 14 Jan 1790
Gough Joseph s William to William Handy 14 Dec 1769 <13 Apr 1775 turned over to Noah Roberts>
Granger Edward s Mary, Leather Lane, Holborn, widow to Henry William Johnson 18 Dec 1833
Granger John s John, Southwark, Sry, glassmaker to Thomas Granger, citizen and merchant tailor 2 Apr 1717
Grant Maurice s Thomas, Bedford Street, Covent Garden, mercer to Francis Cabell 9 Apr 1730
Gray John George s John, Poplar, Mdx, shipwright to Samuel Fenton Read 15 May 1811
Gray William s John† to John Edenbury 18 Jan 1810 <23 Sep 1811 turned over to James Scovell>
Green Charles s Charles, citizen and weaver to Thomas Bracee, citizen and grocer 30 Dec 1697
Green John s Daniel, New Walsingham, Nfk, clerk to Francis Green, cit. & scrivener 2 Nov 1694
Green John s John, St Giles Cripplegate, Mdx, goldsmith† to John Burton 17 Jun 1708
Green Nathan s Nathan, Shoreditch, Mdx, barber to Daniel How 13 Sep 1739
Green Thomas s Richard, citizen and merchant tailor† to Thomas Brock, citizen and merchant tailor 29 Mar 1697 <free>
Greenhalf Godfrey s Thomas, Red Cross Street, sawyer to John Osborne 9 Sep 1736 <14 Sep 1738 turned over to Mary Burton; 11 Feb 1741/2 to Mark Baily>
Greenland John s John, St James Clerkenwell, Mdx, pipemaker to Joseph Blackwell, citizen and blacksmith 2 Apr 1717
Greenley William s William, Beech Lane, Lnd to William Read 13 Mar 1728
Greenly William s William, Lnd to Robert Glyde 8 Jan 1729/30
Greenstreet ... s ... to ... Turner 9 Nov 1781 'omitted'; [*appears after entry for* 9 Nov 1786]
Greenway John s Mary, widow to Mary widow of John Smith, citizen and weaver 8 Jul 1742
Greenwood William s Edward to Charles Lockwood 12 Jul 1764
Gregory Joseph s Joseph, Hitchin, Hrt to John Green 13 Oct 1743
Gregory Marcus s James to James Burnett 10 Jul 1746
Grigg John s Stephen† to Robert Gibbon 11 Jun 1767
Gulliver William s Richard, Petty France, yeoman to Jonathan Sweeting 10 Mar 1736/7 (by charity of Herefordshire Society)
Gumley John s John to Thomas Collins 8 Sep 1763
Gunyon Rowland s Rowland, Banbury, Oxf, vintner to John Walklate 14 Jul 1737
Gyfford John s Anthony, Nuffield, Oxf, clerk to Joseph Kilpin, citizen and goldsmith 22 Oct 1703 <free>

Haddock Thomas s Charles, St John Horsleydown, Sry to David Taylor 13 Sep 1744
Hadfield Frederick s James, Lnd, yeoman to John Churchman 31 Dec 1817
Hagget Samuel s Richard† to John Evans 13 Jun 1745
Haines John s John, citizen and tallow chandler† to Thomas Wagstaff, citizen and merchant tailor 16 Nov 1703 <free>
Haines Thomas s John, Lnd, labourer to George Collise, citizen and haberdasher 6 Oct 1709
Hales Edward s Edward to Catherine How 8 Mar 1753
Hales Edward s Edward to John Read 8 Mar 1770
Hall James s William to Emery ... 14 Jun 1770
Hall John s John, Westminster, Mdx to Ferdinand Richard Camroux 26 May 1829
Hall William s William, St Botolph Aldersgate, coachman† to Benjamin Harris, citizen and broderer 9 Apr 1700 <free>
Hall William s John to William Burrell 12 Oct 1758
Hall William s William† to James Dennis 14 Jan 1768

GOLD AND SILVER WYRE DRAWERS' APPRENTICESHIPS

Halton Samuel s Emanuel, Wingfield Manor, Dby, gentleman to James Huthwait,
  citizen and merchant tailor 16 Aug 1693 <free>
Hammaker Daniel s John to Jonathan Sweeting 14 Aug 1740 (St Margaret Westminster charity)
Hammaker Daniel s Daniel to his father 11 Aug 1768
Hammond Body s John to Sarah Hammond 13 Apr 1769
Hammond Richard s John to James Turner 9 Feb 1764
Handy William s William to Edward Hughs 9 Jul 1747
Hanks John Nightingale s Thomas, New Woodstock, Oxf to Adam Bellinger turned over to
  William Goome, citizen and cordwainer 13 Jun 1776
Hanks Thomas s John, Charlbury, Oxf, cooper to Thomas Pitcher 13 May 1779
Hannam John s John, St James Garlickhythe, Lnd, carpenter to John Duffeild 8 Jul 1725
Hanscomb William s Luke, Clapham, Sry, husbandman to Richard Littlewood,
  citizen and merchant tailor 4 Feb 1717/8
Harding Samuel s John, Windmill Hill, gardener to Samuel Crouch 14 Apr 1726
Hardum Joseph s Joseph, Hadley, Mdx, plumber† to John Read 10 Sep 1778
Harker William s Thomas, citizen and blacksmith to Henry Scatliff, citizen and merchant tailor
  2 Mar 1693/4 <free>
Harmon Edward s Ham, citizen and blacksmith† to Roger Hill, citizen and blacksmith 24 Aug 1697
Harrington Thomas s Samuel, Bristol, clothier to Joseph Harrington, citizen and scrivener
  11 Nov 1718
Harris Andrew s Robert, Woolwich, Ken, master gunner to Stephen Crouch 4 Apr 1836
Harris John s Benjamin, Lnd† to Elizabeth widow of said Benjamin Harris 5 Jun 1716 <free>
Harris Joseph s Samuel, Old Street Road, Mdx, brass founder to George Naylor 11 May 1780
Harris Samuel s Thomas, Newnham, Nth, gentleman to Thomas Bracee, citizen and grocer
  19 Sep 1693 <dead>
✳ Harris Solomon s Jacob, Oat Lane, goldsmith to Joseph Tucker 9 May 1723 <free>
Harris William s Jacob† to Richard Sturley 13 May 1756
Harthaway Benjamin s Benjamin† to Joseph Brown 14 Jan 1762
Hasleden Thomas s John, Wollaston, Nth, gentleman to Daniel Biddle, citizen & weaver 1 Aug 1693
Hasley William s Robert, Woodstock, Oxf, hatbandmaker† to Robert Hussey,
  citizen and longbowstringmaker 7 Dec 1708
Hawkins Edmund s Edmund, Whaddon, Bkm, yeoman to William Gutteridge 22 Apr 1737
  <14 Jan 1741/2 turned over to John Hughes>
Hawkins Richard s Joseph, St Luke, Mdx to Samuel Crouch 8 Aug 1745
Hawkins William s William, Tewkesbury, Gls, yeoman to Richard Smelt 15 Aug 1710 <free>
Hawksworth Thomas s George to John Read 13 Aug 1761
Haye John s John, Bethnal Green, Mdx, weaver to Richard Pugh 18 Jul 1797
Hazard John s Robert, St John Clerkenwell, Mdx, watchmaker to John Read 10 Sep 1778
Hearne James William s William to his father 19 Jan 1805 <23 Sep 1811 turned over to
  George Spearing, citizen and weaver>
Hearne William s Thomas to Robert Gibbon 8 May 1760
Heathcoat Michael s Rowland, Taxal, Chs, gentleman to Roger Longden 16 Jun 1709 <free>
Hemmett William s Christopher, Mortlake, Sry, waterman to William Herne 13 Apr 1775
Hensman John s Michael, Crown Court, Aldersgate Street, tailor to Thomas Cowald 10 Jun 1803
Hensman Joseph s Joseph, Walworth, Sry, yeoman† to Thomas Cowald 9 Dec 1808
Heppell Thomas s Thomas, Westminster, Mdx, mariner to Nathaniel Estwick,
  citizen and longbowstringmaker 13 Dec 1705
Hewett Vincent s Vincent, St Luke, Mdx, weaver to John Underwood 9 Aug 1739
  <9 Jun 1743 turned over to his father>
Hewett William s William, Sparsholt, Ham, yeoman† to ... Turner 26 Jun 1707
Heyfield John s John† to Peter Hammond 7 Apr 1719 <dead>
Higden, Golden Lane, Mdx, rust splitter to Joseph Johnson 16 Dec 1810
Highnam Henry s Henry, citizen and joiner† to Susanna Gascoine widow and blacksmith 4 Sep 1718
Hill George s Richard, Maiden Lane, Covent Garden, Mdx, silversmith† to Goodwin Washbourne
  13 Nov 1735 <7 Jan 1741/2 turned over to ...>
Hill John s George, citizen and merchant tailor† to William Bassom, citizen and merchant tailor
  19 Jul 1706 <free>
Hill Littleton s Littleton† to George Hill 13 Jan 1763

GOLD AND SILVER WYRE DRAWERS' APPRENTICESHIPS

Hill Samuel Harris s Richard, Twickenham, Mdx, perukemaker to Richard Burch 8 Jul 1779
Hill Thomas s George, citizen and merchant tailor† to William Bassom, citizen and merchant tailor 5 Sep 1701 <free>
Hill William s William to Stephen Crouch 8 Nov 1764
Hill William s John, Hornsey, Mdx, farmer† to John Read 13 May 1790
Hiller John s Edward, Bookham, Sry, shoemaker to John Collins, citizen and merchant tailor 24 Aug 1697 <free>
Hiller William s James, St Giles Cripplegate, plumber to Henry William Johnson 7 Jun 1826
Hitchin Ebenezer Priestly s Edward, Shoreditch, Mdx, protestant dissenting minister to Joseph Carter 14 Feb 1771
Hobbs Henry Richard s John to Robert Pitter 10 Aug 1758
Hoddy Robert s Thomas, Clo..., Sfk, dissenting minister to Samuel Crouch 24 Feb 1829
Hollyer Richard s Richard, Falcon Street, Lnd to Michael Doughty 9 Jul 1778
Hollyer William s William, St Botolph Aldersgate, refiner to John Chupsey 11 Nov 1773
Holmes Henry s William, St James Westminster, Mdx, carpenter to George Callis, citizen and haberdasher 4 Feb 1717/8 <14 Nov 1721 turned over to John Smith, citizen and weaver; free>
Holmes Thomas s Thomas, Grub Street, sawyer to Jasper Wilshire 11 Jul 1734 <14 Feb 1739/40 turned over to Francis Houlton>
Holmstead John s Thomas, Cheshunt, Hrt, tailor to Philip Wasburne, citizen and longbowstringmaker 22 Oct 1701
Hopkins William s William to Christopher Cowald 10 Dec 1761
Hotkins Richard s William, Wells, Som, yeoman to Thomas Dawson 20 Aug 1697
Houlton Edward s Charles to Richard Snow 11 Jan 1749/50
Houlton Francis s John, Wokingham, Brk, flaxdresser to John Marlow, citizen and merchant tailor 9 Feb 1726/7
How Daniel s Daniel, Hoxton, Mdx, gardener† to Thomas Mole, citizen and longbowstringmaker 1 Apr 1718 <free>
How John s Michael to Richard Sturley 12 Mar 1761
Howard Henry s William, Market Street, Bdf, scrivener to Hewson Scott 9 May 1745
Howes William s William, Lnd, carman† to George Sewell 8 May 1712 <free>
Hudgson James s James, Ratcliff Cross, Mdx, tallow chandler to William Cowley 19 Sep 1727 <9 May 1728 turned over to Thomas Thame>
Hughes John s William, Wrexham, Den, tanner to Benjamin Negus, citizen and merchant tailor 6 May 1712 <dead>
Hughes John s Edward to his father 13 Aug 1724
Hughes Joseph s John to Isaac Palmer 14 Jul 1763
Hughes Richard s Richard, Bangor, Den to Joseph Harrington, citizen and scrivener 11 Nov 1725
Hughes Thomas s John† to Isaac Palmer 8 Dec 1757
Hughes William s Thomas to James Dennis 12 Apr 1770
Hughes William s ..., Bermondsey, Sry to John Burgin 30 Jul 1830
Hull Samuel s Samuel, Stratford le Bow, Mdx, surgeon to Edward Davis 19 Dec 1717 <15 Dec 1720 turned over to John Gifford>
Humphreys James s James to Thomas Grainger 8 Sep 1768
Hunt Jonathan s Jonathan, citizen and plumber† to John Owen, citizen and longbowstringmaker 5 Mar 1716/7 <4 Jul 1720 turned over to Richard Drury; free>
Hunt Joseph s Joseph, High Wycombe, Bkm, tailor to John Waller 9 Mar 1726/7
Hunt Richard s John, Westminster, Mdx, stonemason to George Burnett 12 Oct 1780
Hunt William s Giles, Ditchside, St Sepulchre, brazier to Walter Crew 4 Aug 1724 <26 Jun 1727 turned over to Edward Langdon, citizen and cordwainer>
Hurdman Edward s Francis, Pirton, Wor, clerk† to Richard Taylor 18 Feb 1698/9 <free>
Hurst Charles s Edward, Red Cross St., Lnd, flatter† to William Gutteridge 20 Sep 1722 <free>
Hurst Owen s Esther Ingram widow of Owen Hurst, St John's Court, grocer† to John Burton 14 Mar 1722/3
Hussey James s John, Carswell Marsh, Buckland, Brk, yeoman to Robert Hussey, citizen and longbowstringmaker 16 Aug 1693 <free>
Hutchcraffe Jane s Mathew to Richard Drury 26 Jul 1712 <free>
Hutchins John s John to Samuel Crouch 8 Oct 1747

GOLD AND SILVER WYRE DRAWERS' APPRENTICESHIPS

Hutchins Philip s Philip, St Giles in the Fields, Mdx, barber to Charles Dennis, citizen and haberdasher 19 May 1699
Huthwaite John s John, Nottingham, Ntt, merchant† to James Huthwaite, citizen and merchant tailor 8 May 1703
Hyder William s William, Grays Inn Lane, barber to Francis Wootton 12 May 1726

Ibbott James s Joseph, Chelsea, Mdx to Henry Johnson Appleford 18 Apr 1821
Iles Marmaduke s Christopher, citizen and draper to Nicholas Cunliffe 14 Jul 1719
Ilsley Thomas s Charles to Robert Gibbon 11 Mar 1762
Ingham William s William, citizen and goldsmith to William Burch 14 May 1772
Ingleby Robert s Thomas, Stamford [? *Ms has* 'Stanfield', Lin], yeoman to William Walton, citizen and armourer 24 May 1695
Ingram Esther *see* Owen Hurst
Inwood John s John, Holborn, Lnd† to William Reeves of Strand 8 Sep 1787
Irons Edward Watson s Moses to George Townsend 9 Jan 1745/6
Isaac Stephen s Sutton, Shoreditch, Mdx, linen draper to John Scarnell 12 Aug 1779

Jackson John s John, St Clement Danes, Mdx, gentleman to John Mady, citizen and goldsmith 3 Aug 1711 <26 Sep 1712 turned over to Nicholas Cunliffe>
Jacob Joseph s William to James Rutland 14 Sep 1752
Jacob Thomas William s William to his father 11 May 1780
Jacob William s William to William Read 8 Nov 1759
Jacobs James s John, White Cross Street, hempdresser to Orme Quarry 9 May 1734
Jakes Nathaniel s Nathaniel to Anna Maria Aylesbury 8 May 1760
James Charles s Hurdman to Charles Lockwood 14 Jan 1762
James William s Thomas to Daniel Butler 13 Dec 1764 <14 Nov 1771 turned over to Thomas Boyce>
Jameson Jonathan s William, Whitechapel, Mdx, gunsmith to Thomas Cowald 13 Jul 1796
Jarvis William s William, St Dunstan in the West, Lnd, carpenter to Richard Pugh 6 Oct 1795
Javan John Thomas s Elizabeth, Hatton Garden, Mdx, widow to Henry Johnson 11 Apr 1821
Javan William s Elizabeth, Hatton Garden, widow to George Edenbury 20 Oct 1822
Javerly Andrew s Andrew to Henry William Johnson 8 Feb 1830
Jefferson Edward s James to John Hughes 11 Oct 1750
Jellico Joseph s Samuel, citizen and innholder to Thomas Chapman, citizen and vintner 4 Dec 1707
Jelliman William s William, Barton, Oxf, husbandman† to Richard King, citizen and merchant tailor 27 May 1701
Jenkins John s Henry, St Botolph Aldgate, Lnd, potter to John Richardson 11 Apr 1771
Jephcott William s Henry, Coventry, War, haberdasher to Daniel Fisher, citizen and cordwainer 3 Sep 1713
Joell Thomas s Thomas, Windsor, Brk, barber† to Thomas Bracey, citizen and grocer 15 May 1702
Johnson Anthony s Anthony, Coleman Street, Lnd, tailor to Samuel Marshall, citizen and merchant tailor 12 Feb 1735/6
Johnson James s James to William Clayton 9 Jul 1767
★Johnson James s Benjamin, Brooks Market, Mdx, butcher to Thomas Cowald 24 Dec 1794
Johnson Joseph s Henry, Shoreditch, Mdx, cordwainer† to Richard Lowther 9 Jun 1774
Johnson Peter s Peter, Snows Fields, Southwark, Sry, painter to Edward Hales 17 Feb 1791
Johnson William s William, Lnd, labourer to Lewis Hurst, citizen and haberdasher 16 Apr 1702
Johnson William s Simon, Marsham Street, Mdx, stone carver† to William James 9 Nov 1795
Jones Charles s John, St Martin in the Fields, Mdx, cordwainer to Pauncefoot Greene 27 Nov 1714
Jones Charles s John, Whetstone, Mdx, farmer to Thomas Taunton 9 Jun 1785
Jones James s Joseph, St George Hanover Square, Mdx, tailor to John Richardson 25 Oct 1804
Jones John s John, Battersea, Sry, baker to Mary Sympson (widow) 11 Jun 1741
Jones Rebecca d John, citizen and glover to Charles Weldon, citizen and merchant tailor 4 Jun 1702
Jones Robert s Robert to John Hammond 10 Mar 1763 (charity of Islington, Mdx)
Jones Robert s Charles, Lambeth, Sry, waterman to William Hemmett 8 Jun 1807
Jones Stephen s Stephen to Thomas Brown 14 Oct 1762
Jones Thomas s John to his father 9 Jun 1768

GOLD AND SILVER WYRE DRAWERS' APPRENTICESHIPS

Jones Valentine s Joseph, St Giles Cripplegate, labourer to John Hughes, citizen and goldsmith 10 Oct 1711
Jones Vaughan Rowland s William to Stephen Goome 12 Apr 1764
Jones Walter s Joseph, Grosvenor Street, Mdx, tailor to John Richardson 18 Jul 1809
Jony Benjamin s Robert to Joseph Brown 13 Dec 1753
Jyles Robert s Brian, St Giles Cripplegate, Mdx, labourer to Joseph Browne 26 Oct 1704

Kellet Henry s Henry† to Daniel Hammacker 13 May 1762
Kelly Abraham s Robert to Stephen Goome 13 Aug 1767
Kent Thomas s Timothy, citizen and wax chandler† to Pauncefoot Green, citizen and ... 28 Jun 1699
Kerby William s Isaac† to John Waller 10 Jun 1762
Kerry John s William to George Vaughan 8 Nov 1744
Keyes John s Thomas, Stony Stratford, Bkm, saddler to Humphrey Baldwin, citizen and goldsmith 10 May 1706 <free>
Kibble Thomas s John† to William Rugby 13 Sep 1744
Kidd Edward s John, Bedford, Bdf, barber to Henry Southouse 2 Dec 1703
Kidley William s Richard, Westminster, Mdx, gardener† to Daniel Featley, citizen and merchant tailor 21 Sep 1698
Kift Henry s Richard, Red Cross Street, poulterer to Richard Drury 14 Apr 1726
Killingley John s Robert, St Giles Cripplegate, wine cooper to William York turned over to Mary widow of William Sympson 14 Sep 1732
King Frederick Henry s Jonathan, St James Westminster, Mdx, stonemason to William Greenwood 11 Jul 1782
King John s Edward† to John Macartney 10 Jul 1760
Kingsley John s William, Mdx, butcher to Henry Hudson 25 Mar 1707
Knight William Frederick s Richard to William Hemmett 23 Jul 1789

Labbee Stephen s Stephen, Mdx, surgeon to Robert Longden 23 May 1706
Laidlow William s ... to Samuel Boston 21 May 1831
Lamb Springett s William, Chipstead, Sry, rector to George Vaughan 10 Nov 1743
Lambert John s John, Pleshey, Ess, blacksmith to George Sewell 31 Jan 1706/7
Lambert Thomas s Zephaniah, St Bride, Lnd, porter to Thomas Pitchers 13 Jun 1782
Lambourne Lazarus s Edward, Old Stratford, Cosgrove, Nth to Joseph Tucker 2 Jul 1711
Lamkin Henry s Henry to John Dawkins 8 Nov 1753
Lampkin Henry s Henry to Daniel How 10 Oct 1754
Lampkin Joseph s Henry to John Hammond 10 Dec 1761
Lancake Joseph s Daniel to Joseph Bowden 14 Aug 1755
Lane Benjamin s Nathaniel, citizen and blacksmith to John Wellsborne, citizen and girdler 3 Dec 1706 <free>
Lane Samuel s John to Mary Burrell 12 Jan 1769 (charity of Buckinghamshire)
Langley James s James to Caleb Potter 14 May 1747
Lashbroke William s Henry† to Francis Houlton 10 Apr 1766
Laxton Martin s Martin, Highgate, Mdx, innholder to Edward Langdon, citizen and cordwainer 6 Sep 1704 <free>
Laxton Martin s Edward, Highgate, Mdx, joiner to William Bassom, citizen and merchant tailor 13 Aug 1724
Lay William s William, Shoreditch, Mdx† to Joseph Johnson 18 Aug 1818 [*paid by* Robert Sewell *uncle of apprentice*]
Leach John s Zachary, Maghull, Lan, clerk to Benjamin Russell, citizen and weaver 15 Aug 1698
Leach John s Thomas to George Rivers 10 Jul 1760
Leach Samuel s Charles, Wem, Sal, apothecary† to William Slane, citizen and cordwainer 27 Sep 1700 <free>
Leadbeater Woodroffe s Robert, St Faith, Lnd, distiller to John Atkinson, citizen and goldsmith 9 Apr 1724
Leadbetter Daniel s James to James Laxton 9 Sep 1756
Leader William s John, Lambeth, Sry, coach painter to John Chapman 5 Jan 1814
Leaver William s Thomas, Shrewsbury, Sal, gentleman to Edward Leaver, citizen and blacksmith 11 Apr 1698 <dead>

GOLD AND SILVER WYRE DRAWERS' APPRENTICESHIPS

Leech James s Charles, Wem, Sal, apothecary† to Edward Hughes, citizen and goldsmith 19 Aug 1706 <free>
Lewington Leshe s Henry Belsher, Stepney, Mdx, gentleman† to Daniel How 9 Mar 1731/2 <14 Dec 1732 turned over to John Whinnell>
Lewis John s William, Covent Garden, Mdx to William Lewis 17 Jan 1822
Lewis John *see also* Edward Edwards
Lewis William s John to William Goome, citizen and cordwainer 11 Sep 1788
Lightfoot William McClary s William Herbert to Samuel McClary 19 May 1826
Lilly Oronoko s Stephen, Ramsgate, Ken, shoemaker† to Charles Lockwood 9 Feb 1775
Ling Charles s Joseph to William Goome 9 Jun 1768
Ling Charles s John to William Goome 8 Jun 1769
Lloyd Thomas s Thomas, Ratcliff, Mdx, mariner† to Richard Roberts 9 Sep 1725 <6 Jan 1728/9 turned over to Nicholas Cunliffe>
Lock Robert s Robert, Chequer Alley, Mdx, smith† to Benjamin Roberts 11 Dec 1800
Lockwood Charles s Benjamin to Samuel Roberts 8 Aug 1751
Loewgear William s Benjamin, Southwark, Sry, barber† to George Sedgewick, citizen and grocer 11 Jun 1707
Long John s Peter to John Munt 11 Jun 1741
Long Robert s Richard, Ruislip, Mdx, husbandman to Walter Ashton 4 Jul 1706
Longden Robert s Anthony, Wormhill, Dby, gentleman† to Edward Page, citizen and haberdasher 27 Apr 1694 <free>
Longden Thomas s Robert to his father 9 Mar 1726/7
Longes Alan s Richard to Thomas Martin 25 Nov 1834
Longland Henry s Elizabeth, St Martin in the Fields, Mdx, widow to Walter Turner 28 Apr 1730
Looker Robert s Robert, citizen and farrier to turned over to Richard Cook, citizen and longbowstringmaker 12 Jul 1708 <free>
Lovejoy Thomas s ..., White Cross Street† to George Wybourne 8 Feb 1738/9 <13 Nov 1740 turned over to John Wale, citizen and cooper>
Lowther Jacob s William, Cripplegate, gentleman to John Gifford 24 Oct 1722 <25 Nov 1725 turned over to William Bird>
※ Lowther Richard s John† to Joseph Carter 10 Oct 1765
Lowther Richard Partridge s Richard to his father 9 Nov 1797

Macartney Thomas s John to Christopher Cowald 13 Aug 1767 <10 Jun 1773 turned over to William King Wigginton>
Maccartney John s John, Westminster, Mdx, yeoman to John Duffeild 12 Nov 1730 <10 Oct 1734 turned over to John Winter>
McClary Henry James s James, Bond Street, Mdx† to Samuel McClary 20 May 1813
McClary Samuel s James, Scotland Yard, Mdx, gentleman† to Thomas Cowald 15 Jul 1790
MacDonald James s William† to Peter Duke 30 Aug 1810
McDonald John s John, Bethnal Green, Mdx, yeoman† to Peter Duke 1 Mar 1814
MacDonald William s John† to Peter Duke 13 Jun 1809
Macdowell John s John, Shoreditch, Mdx, yeoman to Robert Reynolds 23 Sep 1811
McGurk John s Edward to William Banks 9 Jul 1767
Macey John s Robert, Bell Alley, Goswell Street, labourer to Edward Edwards 13 Sep 1733
Macey William s John, Byfleet, Sry, brazier to Robert Glyde 9 Nov 1732
Macey William s Henry† to John Macey 13 Jul 1749
Mackmorran William s William, Newcastle on Tyne, Nbl, haberdasher† to John Cumberledge, citizen and goldsmith 9 Jul 1706
Macleod John s John to William Cotton 11 Jun 1767
Maddox Richard s William, Westminster, Mdx to Samuel Crouch 5 Jul 1715
Mailer William s William, Aldgate, Lnd† to Peter Duke 9 Jun 1796
Mallery Daniel s Daniel, Kenilworth, War, yeoman† to John Burrows 8 Dec 1698 <free>
Mallory John s John, citizen and leatherseller to Daniel Mallory 14 Nov 1722
Malory Daniel s John, Warwick, War, yeoman to Daniel Mallory 1 Dec 1730 <10 Apr 1735 turned over to Robert Wrathall>
Malynes William s William, Newport Pagnell, Bkm† to William Symons 25 Apr 1706
Man Richard s Richard, Lnd, labourer to John Atkinson, citizen and goldsmith 15 Feb 1708/9

GOLD AND SILVER WYRE DRAWERS' APPRENTICESHIPS

Mann John s Edward, Kings Lynn, Nfk, baker to Walter Crew, citizen and longbowstringmaker 27 May 1701 <dead>
Mann Robert s Alexander, Whitefriars to Robert Jones 2 Dec 1825
Manning John s John, Wapping, Mdx to John Whinnell 15 Oct 1723
Manning Mathew s Mathew to James Dennis 9 Jul 1752
Marchant Robert s Robert, Holborn, tailor to William Sansum 10 Jan 1792
Marriot Thomas s John, Old Street, yeoman† to David Taylor 11 Aug 1737
Marsh John s William, Hendon, Mdx, yeoman to William Barnes, citizen and weaver 13 Jul 1698 <free>
Marsh Richard s Gabriel, Grub Street, wiredrawer to his father 11 Feb 1724/5
Marsh Richard s William† to Joseph Brown 14 Jul 1757
Marter William s Thomas, Great Swan Alley, Coleman Street to John Birch 15 May 1828 <13 May 1829 turned over to William Swepson, citizen and blacksmith>
Martin George s Thomas† to James Dennis 13 Sep 1764
Martin John s John, Nayland, Sfk, woolcomber to Jonathan Day, cit. & cordwainer 30 Aug 1700
Martin Joseph s Sarah, Puddle Dock, Lnd, widow to Thomas Pert 8 Oct 1730 <26 Feb 1733/4 turned over to William Jephcaute; 26 May 1736 to Robert Neal>
Marton John s John, Chaldon, Sry, labourer† to George Wybourne 11 Mar 1741/2
Martyne William Cornish s Patience, St Botolph Aldersgate, widow to Thomas Alston 10 May 1739
Mason Joseph s Christopher† to Jonathan Fowler 13 Jun 1765
Mason Martin s Martin to George Naylor 11 Feb 1768
Mason Thomas s Thomas, Lathom, Lan, cooper† to Walter Crew 2 Mar 1708/9
Massingham John s Bryant, Spitalfields, Mdx, yeoman† to Edward Mottrom 10 Apr 1777
Mastin John s Cuthbert, St Margaret Westminster, Mdx, gentleman to Daniel Mallory 14 Nov 1723
Mathews Roger s Mathew, 'Bodwell', Sal, gentleman to Joyce Smith (widow), citizen and haberdasher 18 May 1694 <free>
Matthews William s William to George Rivers 12 Jan 1764
May John s John, Lambeth, Sry, waterman to William Hemmett 14 Sep 1797
May Richard s John (snr.), Lambeth, Sry, waterman to John May (jnr.) 10 Oct 1805
Mayors John s John, Ipswich, Sfk, mariner to William Clayton 12 Jun 1777
Meakins Robert s George to George Wybourn 10 Sep 1719
Meares William s William, Lnd, weaver to Walter Crew 4 May 1714 <free>
Medina *see* De Medina
Megault Richard s Isaac† to Thomas Chapman 9 Feb 1769
Memott Samuel s Edward to William Sympson 12 Sep 1751
Middleton Alexander s John, Durham, clerk† to Peter Brightwell, citizen and blacksmith 3 Apr 1707
Middleton John s Henry, Temple Tysoe, War, yeoman to ... Gutteridge, citizen and longbowstringmaker 10 Jul 1707 <free>
Middleton John s Benjamin, Dagenham, Ess† to Thomas Pierpoynt 12 Dec 1745
Miflin Richard s John to Thomas Shovell 8 Mar 1753
Miles John s John† to Mary Smith 14 Aug 1760
Miles Lewis s John, citizen and gold and silver wyre drawer to his father 14 Dec 1786
Mill John s Norman to John Macartney 13 Mar 1766
Millist James s Thomas, Clerkenwell, Mdx, sawyer† to James Scovell .. Feb 1817
Milne John Kolbe s John, Edinburgh, Sco, commercial agent to Stephen Crouch 15 Nov 1836
Milton John s John† to Edward Mothram 14 May 1767
Mince John s John to Benjamin Roberts 31 Jul 1788
Mitchell Edward Charles s John to Mary Read 14 Jun 1764
Mitchell George s Mary, St Giles Cripplegate, Lnd, widow to John Batson, citizen 2 Dec 1718
Mitchell Thomas s Henry, Pye Street, Westminster, blockmaker† to Thomas Boyce 14 Jan 1779
Mitchell William s William, Edmonton, Mdx, collarmaker to Henry Rivers 13 Mar 1734/5 <14 Dec 1738 turned over to John Betteridge>
Mockett Francis s William, Norton Folgate, Mdx, coal merchant to William Bullmore 18 Jan 1836
Montague Joseph s Joseph, Whaddon, Bkm to Edmund Tanner 16 Nov 1707 <free>
Moore John s John, St Luke, Mdx, tailor to Daniel How 13 Mar 1777 <8 Mar 1781 turned over to Daniel How [*sic*]>
Moore Josiah s John, Red Cross Street, shoemaker to William Gutteridge, citizen and longbowstringmaker 14 Sep 1732

GOLD AND SILVER WYRE DRAWERS' APPRENTICESHIPS

Moore Nathaniel s Thomas, Elford, Sts, clerk to Joseph Harrington, cit. & scrivener 31 Aug 1698
Morgan William s George, Tottenham, Mdx, ironmonger to William Rugby 10 Feb 1736/7
Morris John s Thomas, Lambeth, Sry, haberdasher to Thomas Grainger, citizen and haberdasher 4 Oct 1703 <8 Dec 1708 turned over to John Owen, citizen and longbowstringmaker; free>
Motley John s Thomas, Whaddon, Bkm, labourer to Robert Gascoyne (jnr.) 10 May 1709
Motthram Edward s George to Robert Wrathall 10 Apr 1755
Moult Peter s Daniel, Lnd, cook† to John Fletcher, citizen and grocer 3 Mar 1712/3 <free>
Mountain Robert s Robert to James Burnett 9 May 1754
Mulyneax William s John, Hall Sefton, Lan, yeoman to Benjamin Russell, citizen and weaver 25 Oct 1697 <free>
Mundin James s Thomas to Francis Wilkinson 9 Jun 1757
Munrow James s Walter, Westminster, porter to Charles Matthews, hatbandmaker 25 Oct 1708
Munt John s John, Cranham, Ess, yeoman† to William Shaw 10 Oct 1728

Naish William s ..., St Marylebone, Mdx to George Churchman 10 Oct 1832
Nash James s Edward† to Thomas Grainger 12 Aug 1762
Nash Joseph s John, citizen & blacksmith† to Wandell Winter, citizen & blacksmith 18 Mar 1697/8
Nash Thomas s John, Digswell, Hrt, carpenter to Benjamin Harris, citizen and broderer 28 Jun 1706
Naylor Charles s George to his father turned over to William Hooper, citizen & glover 11 Mar 1779
Naylor George s George to his father 13 Jan 1763
Naylor George William s George to Edward Edwards 9 Oct 1740 (charity of St Luke, Mdx)
Naylor John s George to William Goome 14 Sep 1769
Neal James s Michael, Holborn, Mdx, yeoman to Thomas Cowald 15 Nov 1810
Neat Thomas s Thomas to John Edwards 10 Sep 1761
Nellis James s ... to William Walker 15 Sep 1829
Nelson George s Alexander to Richard Shirley 9 Apr 1767
Nelson William s Alexander to Joseph Jacob 11 Mar 1762
Nesham William s John to James Dennis turned over to William Stackhouse 10 Sep 1767
Newbury William s William to John Macartney 11 May 1749
Newton Joseph s Joseph, citizen and stocking frameworkknitter to Edward Edwards 8 Nov 1744
Newton Thomas s Thomas, Lnd, labourer to Nicholas Cunliffe 14 Apr 1713 <free>
Newton Thomas s Thomas, All Hallows Staining, Lnd, gentleman† to William Harker 13 Jul 1732
Nicholls Walter s Walter to William Dracutt 8 Aug 1751
Nightingale Thomas s Thomas to Stephen Crouch 12 May 1757
Nixon Samuel s Thomas, St Olave Southwark, Sry, baker to John Stanton 4 Sep 1716
Nobbs John s John, Stanstead Abbots, Hrt, yeoman to Arabella Field, citizen and blacksmith (widow) 4 Sep 1705
Norris George William s Thomas to his father 29 Mar 1831
Norris John s John to John Scarnell 9 Feb 1769 <13 Feb 1772 turned over to his father; 12 Nov 1772 to Mary Edwards>
Norris Thomas s Thomas, White Cross Street, Mdx to his father 22 Aug 1796
North John s Aaron† to Richard Miflin 10 Dec 1761
Norton James s John to William Pearsall 11 May 1769 <11 Apr 1771 turned over to Michael Doughty>
Nott Edward s Thomas, Newent, Gls, shoemaker to Edward Davis 10 Mar 1725/6
Nowell Robert s Thomas, St Andrew, Lnd, sawyer to Susanna Clayton 9 Nov 1786
Nowland Thomas s John, Shoreditch, Mdx, carpenter to Francis Cabell 8 Apr 1736

Oately Henry s Hugh, citizen and goldsmith to his father 7 Apr 1704 <free>
Olave Arthur to Lionel Barnes 16 Oct 1722 <free>
Oldham Edward s Thomas, St Giles in the Fields, Mdx, grocer to John Chapman 26 Jun 1811
Orme Samuel s Samuel, Labour in Vain Court, gentleman to Edward Langdon, citizen and cordwainer 12 Aug 1736
Osborne Thomas s John, Lnd to his father 5 Sep 1716
Osborne William s John, Lnd, gold and silver wyre drawer to William Gutteridge, citizen and longbowstringmaker 19 Dec 1717 <free>
Osbourn John s William, Lyme, Dor, mariner† to Thomas Baker 16 Aug 1693
Oswin Henry Plimly s Joseph to David Taylor 13 Aug 1741

GOLD AND SILVER WYRE DRAWERS' APPRENTICESHIPS

Oven Thomas s Henry, citizen and goldsmith to his father 6 May 1707
Owen Edward s Robert, Woolascott [? *Ms has* 'Willcot'], Sal, gentleman to Thomas Chapman, citizen and vintner 20 Jul 1694 <dead>
Owen James s Thomas, Ruislip, Mdx, carpenter† to Alexander Parratt, citizen and merchant tailor 10 Jul 1699

Page John s John, Clerkenwell, Mdx to Thomas Franklyn 8 Sep 1719 <28 Nov 1720 turned over to Richard Hill, citizen and haberdasher; 11 Feb 1724/5 to Thomas Newton>
Palmer Isaac s Isaac, Spitalfields, Mdx, weaver† to Solomon Harris 13 Dec 1744
Palmer Peter s Peter, Bristol, Som, chirurgeon† to Joseph Kilpin, citizen and goldsmith 16 Mar 1693/4 <free>
Palmer William s Robert, Edinburgh, glover to Thomas Perkins, citizen & cook 6 Jul 1696 <free>
Pares John s Elizabeth, Whitechapel, Mdx, widow to John Dodsworth 10 May 1722
Paris Stephen s Stephen to James Dennis 9 Jun 1763
Parker John s Nathaniel, citizen and cordwainer† to Joseph Everett 5 Mar 1716/7
Parker Thomas s Anthony to John Macey 13 Apr 1769
Parkin Henry s George† to John Hammond 13 Nov 1755
Parkin William s Jeremiah to John Hammond 14 Apr 1768
Parsons James s William, Richard St., Commercial Road, brass founder to John Taylor 29 Sep 1828
Parsons Thomas s John, citizen and joiner to John Gifford 3 May 1715
Patt William s Edward, Mdx, cordwainer to William Bassom, citizen and merchant tailor 5 Jul 1704
Patterson Nicholas Francis s Henry† to William Stackhouse 9 Jul 1761
Paxton Michael s William, citizen and pewterer† to John Berkley, citizen and haberdasher 4 May 1708 <free>
Peach William s Robert to James Turner 11 Aug 1757
Peachey Peter s Gregory, Gosport, Ham, gentleman† to Edward Barnes, citizen and merchant tailor 2 Jul 1700 <dead>
Peacock William s John, Cloth Fair, Lnd† to John Maccartney 14 Jun 1744
Peak Daniel s Eleazar, Southwark, Sry to William Simpson 3 Mar 1707/8
Pearkes Richard s John, Stoke Prior, Wor, gentleman to Richard Taylor 11 Jan 1694/5
Pearson William s George, White Cross Street, staymaker to Mark Bailey 13 Sep 1733
Penny Joseph s Joseph, St Dunstan in the West, Lnd, labourer† to Martin Laxton 3 Oct 1716 <19 Oct 1721 turned over to William Hart; 9 May 1723 to William Bassom; free>
Pensom Thomas s Thomas, citizen and haberdasher to his father 5 Jul 1706
Percivall Samuel s John, St Giles in the Fields, Mdx, cooper to Michael Doughty 8 Feb 1776 <11 Dec 1777 turned over to Thomas Cowald>
Pereira Richard s Richard, Aldersgate, hatter to Thomas Pitcher 14 Sep 1780
Persiful James s Thomas† to William Morgan 14 Dec 1749
Pert Thomas s Jonathan, Wotton under Edge, Gls, cordwainer to Walter Crew 12 May 1719 <free>
Pert Walter s Jonathan, Wotton under Edge, Gls, cordwainer to Robert Crew 11 Sep 1729 <8 Jul 1736 turned over to Thomas Pert>
Pessey James s William, Windsor, Brk to Robert Neale 12 Mar 1723/4 <free>
Peters John s Samuel to William Saunders 11 Feb 1762
Peters Robert s William, Barbican, Lnd to Benjamin Roberts 12 Apr 1787
Peters Samuel s Samuel to Joseph Brown 14 Jul 1768
Pevey Isaac s Isaac, citizen and turner to William Turner 10 Nov 1743
Pickeard Thomas s Robert, haberdasher to Michael Heathcote 7 Apr 1719
Picket William s Stephen, St Albans, Hrt, blacksmith to James Burton 12 Dec 1734
Pierpoint Thomas s Francis, Wapping, Mdx, ropemaker to Edward Langdon, citizen and cordwainer 8 May 1729
Pilgrim Joseph s Joseph, Benington, Hrt, yeoman to William Gutteridge, citizen and longbowstringmaker 26 Aug 1708 <free>
Pindar John s John, Fleet Ditch, distiller† to William Simpson 11 Apr 1745
Pingstone Charles s Charles, Holborn, cooper to Edward Hughes 14 Sep 1738 <14 Apr 1743 turned over to Robert Goodchild>
Pinner Thomas s John† to Joseph Brown 12 Aug 1762
Pitcher Thomas s William† to Robert Cox 12 Mar 1767

GOLD AND SILVER WYRE DRAWERS' APPRENTICESHIPS

Pitfeild Robert s ... (did not know his father's name), St Mary Overy Southwark, Sry† to
  Ann Ederingham 13 May 1731 <11 Mar 1735/6 turned over to Samuel Sproston>
Pitter Robert s John, Crawley, Ham, yeoman to Walter Turner 5 Oct 1720 <free>
Plato William James s ... to Edward Stilwell 8 Jan 1824
Platt John s John, Aldersgate Street, dyer† to Edward Langdon, citizen and cordwainer
  14 Feb 1733/4 <8 Feb 1738/9 turned over to John Langdon>
Plumb Samuel s John, Blow Bladder Street, stationer† to Richard Cooke 11 Jan 1732/3
Plumer Francis s Thomas, Bedale, Yks, mercer to Pauncefoot Green 11 Dec 1729
Pollard Robert s Robert, Knutsford, Chs, clothworker† to Richard Littlewood,
  citizen and merchant tailor 20 Nov 1707
Pont Edward s Thomas, Huntingdon, Hun, draper to John Gantom, citizen and goldsmith
  27 Feb 1710/1 <free>
Pope John s Robert, Marnhull, Dor, gentleman to William Gutteridge,
  citizen and longbowstringmaker 14 Jul 1725 <free>
Port Walter s Jonathan, Wotton under Edge, Gls, clothier to Robert Crew 11 Dec 1729
Post Benjamin s Benjamin to John Farr 12 Apr 1753
Potter Caleb s David, Stokesley, Yks, carrier to Richard Smelt 12 Dec 1734 <12 Jul 1739 turned
  over to Joseph Spurr>
Powell John s Edward, Storrington, Ssx, clerk to Robert Glyde 14 Jul 1737
Pratt Thomas s William, St Botolph Aldgate, Mdx, gunsmith to Thomas Cowald 11 Jan 1787
Prest John s George, Ashwell, Hrt, tailor to John Blandfield 10 Jun 1718
Prestland George s George to his father 9 Jan 1723/4 <free>
Preston William s Elizabeth, widow to John Drake 8 Apr 1742
Price Charlton s Mathew, Mgy, gentleman to Robert Crew 8 Dec 1743
Price Mathew s Thomas, citizen and merchant tailor to his father 14 Dec 1702 <free>
Pritchard Samuel s Thomas, St Luke, Mdx, stocking frameworkknitter† to Thomas Brown
  10 Oct 1771 <13 Jun 1776 turned over to Martha Brown>
Pugh Andrew s Roger, citizen and dyer† to William Southouse 4 Jun 1705
Pugh Richard s Richard to Ann Ederingham 10 Aug 1749
Purdom John s Thomas† to James Laxton 13 May 1762

Quantiteau Henry s Peter, St Martin in the Fields, gentleman† to John Dodsworth 11 Apr 1734
Quarles Daniel s Daniel, Lnd, butcher† to William Simpson 12 Nov 1714 <free>
Quarry Orme s William, citizen and cordwainer to Catherine Winstone, widow and clothworker
  17 Oct 1710 <free>
Quested Henry s Robert, Cripplegate, spinner to Richard Littlewood 16 Oct 1722 <17 May 1727
  turned over by Richard's execs. to John Ford, citizen and cordwainer>
Quillingborough John s Henry, Kettering, Nth, gardener to Peter More, citizen and blacksmith
  27 Oct 1698 <dead>

Raevisse Henry s Thomas, Shefford [? in Ms 'Sherperd'], Bdf, labourer† to Richard Smelt
  11 Sep 1718 <free>
Raper Benjamin s Henry, Fringill [? in Ms 'Fringhall'], Yks to Richard Roberts 6 Mar 1718/9
Rare Thomas s Thomas, Richmond, Sry, fisherman† to Thomas Gardner, citizen and fishmonger
  3 Mar 1712/3 <dead>
Read Benjamin s Thomas, Tower Street, Lnd, turner† to John Waller 12 Feb 1735/6
Read Eli s John, Mdx, cordwainer to William Balsam, citizen and merchant tailor 1 Jul 1718
  <19 Apr 1722 turned over to Elizabeth Clark (widow)>
Read Henry s John, citizen and weaver to Roger Hill, citizen and blacksmith 7 Aug 1701
Read John s Thomas to Elizabeth Davis 14 Nov 1751
Read William s John, Appleton le Moors, Yks, yeoman to Susanna Josephs (widow) 2 Aug 1711
Read William s Thomas to William Read 9 May 1754
Reader Edward s William, Maidstone, Ken, labourer to John Churchman 7 Apr 1829
Record Bedford s Henry to James Rutland 12 Jun 1746
Reeve George s William† to Joseph Atkinson 13 Jul 1749
Reeve Thomas s Thomas, Hertford, Hrt, tailor to John Reeve, citizen and blacksmith 12 Dec 1723
Reeves Edmund s John to Thomas Pitcher 12 Jun 1788
Reeves William s Thomas† to John Gifford 10 Aug 1758

GOLD AND SILVER WYRE DRAWERS' APPRENTICESHIPS

Regneir John s Andrew to James White 10 Jan 1753
Reminton Benjamin s Michael, St Giles Cripplegate, labourer† to Edward Finch, citizen and weaver 19 Jun 1701
Reynolds Ebenezer s Ebenezer to Sarah Burnett 14 May 1761
Reynolds James s Robert to his father 14 Feb 1811
Reynolds Joseph s Robert, Thaxted, Ess, shoemaker to Henry Quested 8 Aug 1745
Reynolds Robert s Cuffyn, St Giles Cripplegate, Lnd, cordwainer to William Clayton 13 Jul 1775
Rice Edward s Edward† to Henry Questead 11 Jun 1761
Richards John s Thomas, Enfield, Mdx, chandler to Edward Hughs, citizen and goldsmith 12 Nov 1730
Richardson George s Henry, Labour in Vain Court, Lnd, porter to Joseph Johnson 29 Aug 1806
Richardson James s Joseph to Robert Wrathall 14 Feb 1760
Richardson John s Alexander to Joseph Carter 13 May 1762
Richardson Richard s John to William Howes 14 Feb 1750/1
Richardson Samuel s Joseph to George Naylor 12 Jun 1766
Richardson Thomas s John, Shadwell, Mdx, mariner† to Elizabeth widow of Robert Gascoyne (jnr.) 3 Dec 1714
Richardson Zachariah s Thomas to James Laxton 8 Nov 1750
Rider Jacob s Thomas, Strand, Mdx, gentleman to John Chupsey 15 Jan 1790
Ridgwick Edward s William, St Giles Cripplegate, hatter to Robert Longden 5 Mar 1716/7
Riell Robert s Robert, St John Westminster, Mdx to Thomas Washbourne 14 Apr 1743
Ring Henry s Henry, Devizes, Wil, gent.† to John French, cit. & currier 10 Aug 1694 <dead>
Rivers George s Mordecai to Hewson Scott 14 Jul 1743
Rivers Thomas s Mordecai to Hewson Scott 13 Mar 1755
Roberts James s John, Chelsea, Mdx, tailor to Lionel Barnes 12 Mar 1723/4 <gone to sea>
Roberts John s Joshua, citizen and feltmaker† to Charles Underwood, citizen and weaver 2 May 1699 <free>
Roberts John s Noah to Henry Turner 10 Apr 1783
Roberts John s John, St Luke, Mdx, yeoman to Richard Pugh 12 Jun 1806
Roberts John Joseph s John, Spitalfields, Mdx† to Thomas Joseph Andrews 18 Oct 1814 <14 Aug 1816 turned over to ...>
Roberts Richard s John, citizen and haberdasher to Nicholas Cunliffe 20 Nov 1707 <free>
Roberts Sarah d Thomas, Rodborough, Gls, clothier to James Douglas, citizen and vintner 9 Apr 1724 <free>
Roberts William s Noah to William Turner 13 Jul 1786
Roe William s John, Lnd, labourer to Thomas Burgett, cit. & fishmonger (brushmaker) 5 Aug 1719
Rogers George s John, Bloomsbury, Mdx, gentleman to Jasper Wiltshire 14 Jul 1737
Rogers Richard s John, St Nicholas Worcester, Wor, yeoman to John Atkins, citizen and goldsmith 17 Sep 1705
Rosher George s John, Bethnal Green, Mdx to John Churchman 15 Jun 1821
Rowland Hugh s William, 'Sandiston', Cae, labourer to John Wainwright 14 Oct 1725 <14 Nov 1728 turned over to Robert Glyde>
Rudd Thomas s Thomas, Shoreditch, Mdx, gentleman† to Edward Page, citizen and haberdasher 29 Nov 1698 <dead>
Rugby Thomas s Thomas, citizen and cooper to William Symonds 8 Apr 1725
Rugby William s Thomas, Lnd, cooper to Richard Hill, citizen and haberdasher 6 Jul 1714 <free>
Russell John s John to William Stackhouse 8 Jun 1769

Sabra Lewis William s Lewis William, mariner to George Burnett 13 Feb 1777 (charity of St Margaret Pattens, Lnd)
Salmon John s John, Nbl† to William Harker 29 Aug 1739
Salter Edward s Richard, St Sepulchre, Lnd, wiredrawer to Elizabeth Parkins 14 Feb 1771 <9 Jul 1772 turned over to Charles Bull>
Salter Richard s Richard to John Waller 13 Nov 1740
Samman Richard s John to Samuel Dawkins 8 Oct 1761
Sanders William s Stracey to Henry Questead 10 Sep 1767 <13 Sep 1770 turned over to Mary Questead; 14 May 1772 to Mary Edwards>
Sansum William s William to William Clayton 9 Nov 1769

GOLD AND SILVER WYRE DRAWERS' APPRENTICESHIPS

Sapp Stephen s Richard, Southwark, Sry, compass maker to Stephen Roberts, citizen and longbowstringmaker 8 May 1707 <dead>
Saul Charles s Charles to Francis Wilkinson 10 Jul 1760
Saunders John s Richard to John Turner 13 Oct 1768
Saunders Robert s William to Henry Questead 9 Dec 1756
Saunders Stephen s William, Grub Street, weaver to John Snow 12 Jul 1733 <11 Mar 1735/6 turned over to Andrew Aylesbury>
Saunders William s William, Crowderswell Alley, Cripplegate, weaver to Robert Crew 10 Jun 1725 <free>
Saunders Zachariah s William to his father 14 Jul 1757
Savage Joseph s James, St Mary Axe, Lnd, yeoman to John Turner 21 Jun 1795
Savory Henry s Henry to John Hughes 11 May 1758
Saxby James s James, Sudbury, Sfk, silk dyer to Thomas Martin 22 Mar 1836
Sayer Thomas s Thomas, St Giles in the Fields, Mdx, painter† to Anthony Sparrow 23 Mar 1795
Sayes William s Thomas† to William Morgan 10 Jan 1750/1
Scales Charles s John, Spitalfields, Mdx, ropemaker to David Strong 9 Jun 1726 <3 Mar 1728/9 turned over to Thomas Atwood>
Scarnell John s Thomas to James Dennis 12 Jul 1753 (charity of Thetford, Nfk)
Scott Charles s Hewson to his father 11 Feb 1741/2
Scott Hewson s John, Shields, Nbl, mariner† to John Dawkins 4 Sep 1716 <free>
Scott John s George, Lnd, yeoman† to Edward Davies 26 Jul 1802
Scott Samuel s Richard, St Martin in the Fields, gent.† to Richard Taylor 27 Feb 1718/9 <at sea>
Scovell James s Robert, Southampton, Ham, mariner to Richard Birch 13 Feb 1794
Seagood Joseph s John, citizen and carpenter† to William Osborne, citizen and armourer 25 Apr 1699 <free>
Seares Thomas s Thomas, citizen & leatherseller to Benjamin Russel, citizen & weaver 3 Jun 1706
Searles John s Clement, citizen & merchant tailor to Joseph Atkins, cit. & goldsmith 30 May 1711
Seddon John s John to John Green 9 May 1765
Sedgwick William s George, Lnd, grocer to John Hughes, citizen and goldsmith 5 Jul 1715
Sell James George s James, Bunhill Row, yeoman† to Henry Deeves .. Dec 1808
Senecal Ezekias s John to Ezekias Paxton 26 Aug 1748
Sharp John s Richard† to Robert Wrathall 8 Jan 1761
Sharp Richard s Richard, Rotherhithe, Sry, waterman to Samuel Crouch 13 Dec 1722
Sharpe Francis s Winifred, Bloomsbury Market, Mdx, widow to Richard Drury turned over to Thomas Sharpe, citizen and haberdasher 15 May 1727
Shaw Charles s John, Brentford, Mdx, victualler† to Thomas Gardner, citizen and fishmonger 4 Apr 1706 <free>
Shaw Edward s Julius, White Cross Street, tailor to William Shaw 8 Nov 1733
Shaw James s Robert, Red Cross Street, brewer to John Court 11 Dec 1735
Shaw William s Julius, citizen and merchant tailor to George Callis, citizen and haberdasher 5 Apr 1706 <free>
Sheapherd James s Robert, Shrewsbury, Sal, mercer to Nathaniel Smith, cit. & grocer 25 Jul 1696
Shepcutt William s Edward to John Studdard 9 Jun 1768
Shepheard Philip s William to Henry Allcraft 9 Apr 1747
Shepherd John s John, Mdx, labourer to Robert Questwood, cit. & broderer 14 Feb 1703/4 <free>
Shepherd John s Abraham to William Read 14 Aug 1746
Shepperd James s William to Philip Shepperd 11 Aug 1757
Sherman Feutrall s Feutrall, Newgate Street, Lnd† to Joseph Tucker 8 Apr 1736 <9 Oct 1740 turned over to Thomas Collins>
Shields James s Thomas to Michael Doughty 13 Sep 1764
Shipman Isaac s Isaac† to Lewis Miles 13 Jun 1799
Shirley Jeremiah s John† to Edward Davis 8 Jan 1756
Shirley Joseph s John, Stow, Bkm, glazier to Edward Davis 11 Feb 1724/5
Shovell Thomas s John, Petticoat Lane, weaver to Thomas Reeve 13 May 1736
Silvester John s Philip, Fore Street, watchmaker to Robert Neal 11 Mar 1724/5
Simmons Peter s Elias, Grub Street, Lnd, surgeon to William Goome 13 Apr 1780
Simonds Thomas s Samuel, Wick, Wor, gent. to John Lane, cit. & weaver 25 Dec 1695 <dead>
Simpcock Mathew s Mary, Dunings Alley, Bishopsgate St., widow to Benjamin Goffe 11 Jul 1728

GOLD AND SILVER WYRE DRAWERS' APPRENTICESHIPS

Simpson Thomas s Edward to John Hughes 2 Sep 1752
Slader Samuel s John, Watford, Hrt, doctor of physic to Thomas Brock, citizen and merchant tailor 13 Oct 1705
Small James s James, St Martin in the Fields, tailor to William Southouse 9 Jan 1723/4 <dead>
Smallwood Thomas s Thomas, Fore Street, carman† to William Sympson 10 Feb 1725/6 <free>
Smedly Thomas s Thomas, Lnd, weaver to John Burton, citizen and goldsmith 17 Jul 1710
 <1 Sep 1713 turned over to John Atkinson, citizen and goldsmith>
Smelt Richard s Richard to his father 13 Jan 1723/4 <free>
Smith ... s ...† to Henry Sparrow 1 May 1828
Smith Benjamin s Benjamin, Pimlico, Mdx, tailor to John Richardson 18 Nov 1796
Smith Daniel s Stephen to William Evans 13 Aug 1747
Smith Edmund Thomas s Edmund, Greenwich, Ken to John Burgin 19 May 1826
Smith George s Thomas, Aldgate, Lnd, tide waiter to Lionel Barnes 19 Jan 1702/3 <free>
Smith John s Thomas, Woburn, Bkm, barber to William Gutteridge, citizen and longbowstringmaker 20 Apr 1730
Smith John s Mary, Clerkenwell, Mdx, widow to Anthony Sparrow 13 Jul 1820
Smith Mark s Mark, St Giles in the Fields, Mdx, tailor to Edward Langdon, citizen and cordwainer 10 Feb 1731/2
Smith Reuben s Reuben, Crooked Lane, Lnd, wine merchant to Samuel Fenton 3 Aug 1813
Smith Richard s Richard, citizen and vintner to Thomas Buswell, citizen and longbowstringmaker 4 Dec 1707
Smith Richard s Richard, Exeter, Dev, yeoman to John Atkinson, citizen and goldsmith 10 Jan 1716/7 <free>
Smith Richard s Elizabeth, Pouls Alley, widow to Mark Bailey 11 Dec 1729 <12 Jun 1735 turned over to Jonathan Sweeting>
Smith William s Henry to Mary Smith 11 Dec 1766
Smith William s Mary, Clerkenwell, Mdx, widow to Anthony Sparrow 24 Jan 1821
Smith William s William to Robert Willin 12 Aug 1824
Smith William Haddon s William, Drury Lane, Mdx, gentleman† to Edward Edwards 8 Oct 1810
Smith William John s William, Bethnal Green, Mdx, painter† to Richard John Birch 28 Oct 1826
Snape Nathaniel s Robert, St Bride, Lnd, weaver to William Shaw 9 Sep 1731
Snow John s Richard, citizen & stationer to William Barnes, citizen & weaver 29 Sep 1701 <free>
Snow Richard s John to his father 12 Nov 1730
Southouse Thomas s William to his father 25 Nov 1725
Sparrow Anthony s Anthony to Simon Sparrow 9 Apr 1761
Sparrow John s Anthony† to his brother Anthony Sparrow 13 Oct 1768
Sparrow Simon s Simon, Bedale, Yks to Jonathan Sweeting 10 May 1744
Spencer Henry s Henry to William Turner 14 Aug 1746
Spencer John s Edward, Clerkenwell Green, Mdx, bitmaker to John Gifford 14 Oct 1736
Spencer William s William, Aldersgate Street, yeoman to Nicholas Cunliffe 14 Sep 1732
Spittle Charles s Charles to Andrew Aylesbury 14 Aug 1746
Sproston Samuel s Robert, Shoe Lane, Mdx, founder† to Mark Bailey 10 May 1722 <free>
Stancefield John s John† to William Goome 9 Feb 1758
Stanley Samuel s John, Clerkenwell, Mdx, tailor to Thomas Pitcher 17 Sep 1790 <9 Nov 1792 turned over to Benjamin Roberts>
Stapleton Samuel s Richard, Keysoe, Bdf, yeo. to Daniel Day, cit. & merchant tailor 2 Feb 1702/3
Stapleton Samuel s John, St Botolph Aldersgate, engine weaver to William Sansum 3 Jun 1800
Starke John s Joseph, citizen and cordwainer† to Richard Cooke 7 Nov 1712
Stead George s George, citizen and mercer to John Blatchford, citizen and goldsmith 22 May 1729
Stephens John s William, Chippenham, Wil, innholder to Edward Hughes, citizen and goldsmith 14 Jan 1736/7 <14 Jan 1741/2 turned over to John Ford>
Stephenson John s Benjamin to Thomas Brown 13 Jan 1757
Stevenson Nathaniel s Benjamin, St Giles in the Fields, Mdx, labourer to John Atkinson, citizen and goldsmith 30 Dec 1697
Stillwell Edward s Jane, Southwark, Sry, widow to Daniel Atherley 11 Oct 1802
Stoddard John s John, Golden Lane, cutler† to William Gascoyne 8 Aug 1734
Strange John Briscoe s John, Aldersgate Street, Lnd, glass cutter† to Lewis Miles 9 Dec 1802
Strong David s Ralph, cit. & gold and silver wyre drawer to Robert Neal 10 Mar 1713/4 <free>

GOLD AND SILVER WYRE DRAWERS' APPRENTICESHIPS

Stubbs Joseph s John, Old Street, Mdx, chairmaker to Lewis Charles Miles 16 Oct 1809
Sumner Jacob s John, St Giles Cripplegate, Mdx, labourer to Nathaniel Lane, citizen and blacksmith 16 Feb 1704/5
Sutton John s Samuel, Toddington, Bdf, baker to Warner Wenham, citizen and longbowstringmaker 13 Jul 1732
Swane John s Thomas, cit. & joiner to James Parratt, cit. & merchant tailor 16 May 1699 <free>
Sweeting Henry s Henry, Bristol, Gls, ropemaker to Nathaniel Butler, citizen and longbowstringmaker 12 May 1737 <12 Apr 1739 turned over to Joseph Burton>
Sweetting Jonathan s Jonathan, Kelvedon, Ess, maltster to John Joseph 6 Dec 1704 <free>
Swift Godfrey s Godfrey to George Townsend 9 Nov 1769

Tanner Edmund s Edmund, Coggeshall, Ess, grocer to Benjamin Negus, citizen and merchant tailor 13 May 1698 <free>
Tatum Edward s William† to William Read 13 Oct 1768
Tatum Thomas s William to James Dennis 8 May 1746
Tatum William s William to Thomas Tatum 14 Aug 1760
Tatum William s Thomas to his father 8 Mar 1781
Taunton Thomas s John to Francis Wilkinson 11 Apr 1745
Taylor David s Edward, Bangor, Den to John Burton 7 Feb 1715/6 <free>
Taylor Isaac s John, East Grinstead, Ssx, yeoman to George Wybourne 14 Jul 1726
Taylor John s Robert to John Walklate 9 Jun 1763
Taylor Richard s Richard, Hornchurch, Ess, yeoman† to John Maddey, citizen and merchant tailor 8 Jan 1707/8
Taylor Thomas s Edward, Bangor, Den to Edward Hughes, cit. & goldsmith 29 Apr 1710 <free>
Taylor Thomas s Thomas, Castle Lane, Southwark, Sry, yeoman to Daniel How 13 Nov 1735
Terry William s James, Walthamstow, Ess, yeoman to Richard Birch 3 Aug 1799
Tew Henry s William, Chick Lane, Lnd† to Thomas Cowald 10 Oct 1800
Thames Thomas s Thomas, Sts, husbandman to William Harker 3 Feb 1718/9 <free>
Thomas Edmund s Edmund to Robert Pitter 11 Apr 1754
Thomas Henry s Henry, citizen and merchant tailor† to Arabella Field, citizen and blacksmith (widow) 20 Aug 1697
Thomas William s Francis, Covent Garden, Mdx, shoemaker to Henry Lovelace, citizen and haberdasher 18 May 1694 <free>
Thompson John s William, Doctors Commons, Lnd, gentleman to William Harker 8 Jul 1731
Thompson John s George† to John Macey 12 Dec 1765
Thornton Richard s Richard, Lnd, labourer† to Richard Blake 24 Apr 1701 <free>
Tillinghast Stephen Atton s John to David Taylor 30 May 1754
Timms John s William, Bow, Mdx, labourer to Thomas Mole, citizen and longbowstringmaker 5 Sep 1706
Tinkler Guy s Guy, Barnards Castle, Dur, tailor to Arabella Field, citizen and blacksmith (widow) 8 May 1699 <free>
Tipper Geoffrey s William, Lnd† to Thomas Alston 12 May 1737
Tipper John s John, St Giles Cripplegate, Lnd, labourer to John Bacon, citizen and longbowstringmaker 20 Dec 1709 <6 Mar 1715/6 turned over to John Dodsworth; free>
Tofield Thomas s Thomas to Thomas Brown 14 May 1767
Toger Richard s Alexander, Bermondsey, Sry, shoemaker to Edward Hales 12 Apr 1796
Tomkins James s Thomas† to Richard Salter 8 Mar 1749/50
Tooley Thomas s John, Old Street, mason† to Edward Langdon, citizen and cordwainer 14 Oct 1725
Tosier Peter s Peter, Salisbury, Wil, yeoman to John Embry 8 May 1740
Townsend George s George, Shoreditch, Mdx, labourer to John Reeve, citizen and blacksmith 8 Jul 1731 <8 Aug 1734 turned over to Mary Sympson (widow)>
Townsend George s George† to James Burnett 12 Jun 1755
Tringham William s Thomas, Clerkenwell, Mdx to Henry Johnson Appleford 2 May 1825
Trueman John s Robert, Frome, Som, clothier to John Betteridge 13 Nov 1740
Truscoat George s James, Spitalfields, Mdx, jeweller to John Edenbury 23 Apr 1804
Tunstall Edward s Anthony, St Sepulchre, Mdx, cabinet maker to John Miles 21 Oct 1791
Turbutt Benjamin s Francis, Barbican, Lnd, watchmaker to Thomas Brock (jnr.) 8 Nov 1722
Turner Francis s James to his father 11 Dec 1760

GOLD AND SILVER WYRE DRAWERS' APPRENTICESHIPS

Turner Francis s Francis to his father 12 Jul 1791
Turner James s Francis, White Cross Street, wiredrawer to William Turner 13 Jun 1734
Turner James s Francis, citizen and gold and silver wyre drawer† to Anthony Sparrow 31 Aug 1807
Turner John s William† to John Green 14 Jun 1759
Turner John s William, St Giles Cripplegate, Lnd to his father 10 Oct 1776
Turner John s John to his father 12 Jun 1788
Turner John Lindsey s William, Portsmouth, Ham, wheelwright† to William Turner 9 Jan 1772
Turner Samuel s John, St Giles Cripplegate, spinner to Jeremiah Walton, citizen and blacksmith
    14 Oct 1725 <8 Jan 1729/30 turned over to William Gascoyne>
Turner William s William, Poor Jury Lane, Lnd, farrier to Edward Hughes 17 Jan 1722/3
Turner William s William† to John Green 9 Apr 1747
Turney Charles s John to Thomas Shovell 13 Apr 1749
Turnham William s Thomas to John Read 12 Aug 1762
Turville Thomas s Henry, St Martin in the Fields, Mdx, milliner to John Lane, citizen and weaver
    15 Feb 1704/5
Tutin Ann d John to Anthony Norman 14 Jul 1763
Tuttle Richard s Thomas, citizen and turner to John Bacon, citizen and longbowstringmaker
    10 Feb 1701/2 <free>
Tyson Peter s Thomas to Richard Burch 13 Apr 1769

Uffington John s John to William Turner 10 Oct 1765
Underwood John s Thomas, Maulden, Bdf, gardener to Joseph Tucker 30 Oct 1719
Underwood Richard s Thomas, citizen and ...† to Benjamin Roberts 5 Jun 1800
Underwood Thomas s George to John Underwood 14 Dec 1758
Underwood William s John to his father 14 Oct 1762
Usher Howard s James, Vine Street, Westminster, Mdx, gentleman to John Whinnell 13 Dec 1733
Uzuld John s William, St Giles Cripplegate, shoemaker to John Pilgrim turned over to
    Thomas Prosser, citizen and merchant tailor 19 Jan 1720/1

Vaughan Charles s Robert, Holborn, Lnd, carpenter† to William Hughes 14 May 1789
Vaughan George s James, 'Delamare', Hef, yeoman to Richard Tayler 13 Apr 1727
Vaux William s William, citizen and longbowstringmaker to Julius Berrisford, citizen and weaver
    24 Feb 1703/4 <free>
Vesey William s John, Tooley Street, Southwark, Sry, brewer to Richard Drury 11 Feb 1724/5
Villepierre William s Paul to Thomas Tatum 13 Aug 1767
Virtue William Henry s Benjamin, Chelsea, Mdx, victualler to Richard Lowther 14 Feb 1782
Vokins William s John, St Sepulchre, Lnd, yeoman to John Whinnell 12 Aug 1731

Wade Thomas s Thomas, Mitcheldean, Gls, gentleman† to Jonathan Cooke, citizen and ironmonger
    25 Jun 1696
Wainwright John s Gabriel, Lnd, glover† to Richard Grenway, citizen and longbowstringmaker
    30 May 1698 <free>
Walker Joseph s Joseph, Kirby Street, Mdx, jeweller† to Thomas Chapman 9 Oct 1799
    <16 Jan 1804 turned over to John Chapman>
Walker Robert s Robert, Leg Alley, Long Acre, Mdx, yeoman to Thomas Pitchers 7 Oct 1789
Walker Thomas s Isaac, Windsor, Brk† to Thomas Bracey, citizen and grocer 1 Dec 1704 <free>
Walker William s John, Cheshunt, Hrt, grocer to Samuel Percival 2 Nov 1812
Walkingame Francis s John, Bloomsbury, Mdx, gentleman to Walter Turner 9 Jun 1737
Walklate John s Thomas, citizen and plumber to Daniel Mallery 19 Dec 1710 <free>
Wall Henry s Thomas, Goodmans Fields, Whitechapel, Mdx, clothworker to William Harker
    27 Apr 1721 <discharged>
Waller John s ... to Peter Hamond 22 Dec 1713 <free>
Walpoole William s William, Willesden, Mdx, victualler to Thomas Brock,
    citizen and merchant tailor 13 Sep 1700
Walsh Thomas s David, Dublin, Ire, merchant to Francis Greene, citizen and scrivener 11 Jun 1702
Walter Samuel s Charles, Kensington, Mdx, yeoman to Anthony Sparrow 14 Jan 1790
Walton John s John, citizen and goldsmith to his father 9 Mar 1698/9
Warburton William s William, Lnd, watchcasemaker to William Harker 18 Mar 1714/5

GOLD AND SILVER WYRE DRAWERS' APPRENTICESHIPS

Ward John s John, Grub Street, Lnd† to James Scovell 29 Dec 1805
Ward Vincent s Francis, Mdx, hempdresser to Joseph Blackwell, citizen and blacksmith 1 Aug 1706
Ward Walter s John, Coleshill, War, mercer to John Dodsworth 13 Aug 1730
Warner John s John to Daniel How 11 May 1769
Warner Joseph s William, Stroud, Gls, yeoman to William Reeves 14 Jun 1802 <18 Nov 1803 turned over to Joseph Wood, citizen and turner>
Warner Richard s William, Stroud, Gls, clothworker to William Reeves 10 Jan 1792
Warner William s William, Stroud, Gls, clothier to William Reeves 4 Apr 1793
Warrand Christopher s Thomas, St Martin in the Fields, Mdx, tailor to Thomas Mathew, citizen and grocer 31 Mar 1699
Warren Dominic s Miles† to Joseph Allen 11 Apr 1765
Warren John Thomas s Thomas, citizen and joiner to John Wescott 11 Oct 1744
Warren Robert s Miles† to Robert Wrathall 10 Mar 1763
Warren William s Francis, Hutton le Hole, Yks† to John Whilton, citizen and weaver 9 Jan 1706/7
Warrington Richard s John, St Giles Cripplegate, weaver to Joseph Everett, citizen and haberdasher 22 Mar 1707/8
Washborne Thomas s Goodwin to his father 14 Nov 1723
Washburn Goodwin s William, St Giles Cripplegate, Lnd, labourer to Philip Wasshburn, citizen and longbowstringmaker 18 May 1694 <free>
Washington John s Thomas† to Sarah Shovell 14 Jun 1759
Watkins John s Charles, Moreton, Ess, yeoman to Robert Berkley, citizen and merchant tailor 15 Jul 1698 <free>
Watkins John s Richard, Madley, Hef, yeoman to Benjamin Russell, citizen and weaver 10 Oct 1705
Watmough Edmund s Edmund, Newington, Sry, mariner to Richard Smelt 14 Oct 1725 <free>
Watson George s William, Suffolk Street, East Blackman Street to John Churchman 2 Feb 1825
Watts George Edward s George, Earl Street, Blackfriars† to Henry Deeves 7 Mar 1814
Way Ambrose s Charles, Minories, gunsmith to Thomas Prosser, citizen and merchant tailor 14 Aug 1729
Webb James s James to Thomas Shovell 11 Jun 1752
Webb John s John to Francis Houlton 9 Nov 1749
Webb Thomas s James, White Cross Street, St Luke, Mdx, smith to Anthony Sparrow 11 Jan 1776
Webb William s James, Castle Town, Isle of Man, gentleman to Thomas Chapman 9 Jul 1778
Webster Solomon s Solomon† to Stephen Crouch 14 Apr 1768
Welch William s Oliver to William Goome 8 Apr 1762
Wells Nathaniel s Joseph, Cheltenham, Gls, hatter and bookseller to Christopher Cowald 12 May 1774 <18 Nov 1774 turned over to Thomas Cowald>
Wells William s David, Bermondsey, Sry, gardener to Richard Tozer 15 Jun 1803
Welsh James s George† to Daniel How 10 Dec 1761
Wenham George s Thomas, citizen and longbowstringmaker to his father 8 Aug 1706 <free>
West Francis s Francis, Holborn, Mdx, gardener to Thomas Bracee, citizen and grocer 1 Jul 1700
Westcoat John s ... to Humphrey Baldwin 26 Sep 1714 <17 Dec 1718 turned over to Robert Glyde; free>
Westcott John s John to his father 11 Aug 1737
Weyman James s James, White Cross Street, yeoman to Thomas Cowald 1 Aug 1810
Wheatly James s James to William Farr 11 Apr 1754
Wheatly John s Joseph to James Wheatly 8 Apr 1762
Wheeler Thomas s Thomas, St Mary Cray, Ken, glover to William Barnes, citizen and weaver 15 May 1707
Whitchurch William s William, Great Horwood, Bkm, farrier to William Dandridg, citizen and blacksmith 7 Apr 1698
White George s John, Dukes Court, St Martins Lane, Mdx to George Edward Watts 19 Jan 1827
White James s George, Christ Church, Ham, saddler† to Joseph Tucker 9 Sep 1731
White John s Thomas, citizen and turner to Benjamin Jennings 15 Aug 1710 <dead>
White John s John† to Noah Roberts 14 May 1767
White Lewis s Lewis, Cheshunt, Hrt, woolcomber to Philip Washburn, citizen and longbowstringmaker 7 Nov 1700
White Thomas s Edmund, St Giles Cripplegate, Mdx, bricklayer to Thomas Pitcher 10 Apr 1777
White William s Esther, widow to William Jephcoate 14 May 1741

GOLD AND SILVER WYRE DRAWERS' APPRENTICESHIPS

Whitehead Thomas s Thomas, Moor Lane, sawyer to Joseph Everett, citizen and haberdasher 11 Feb 1724/5
Whiting Timothy s Timothy, Fetter Lane, St Dunstan in the West, Lnd, coppersmith to William Howes 12 May 1737
Whynnell John s Paul, Bridport, Dor, husbandman† to Robert Gascoyne, citizen and blacksmith 23 Mar 1702/3 <free>
Wieland William s John, St Luke, Mdx, watchmaker to Edward Davis 13 Jun 1782
Wiggins Thomas s John, Witney, Oxf, blanket maker to Samuel Roberts turned over to William Stackhouse 14 Sep 1774
Wigginton William King s William to John Macartney 13 Oct 1763
Wild Michael s William, Clerkenwell, Mdx, labourer† to Joseph Blackwell, citizen and blacksmith 9 Jun 1719 <transported>
Wilder Thomas s Isaac, Islington, Mdx, bricklayer to Richard Birch 5 Jul 1797
Wilding Samuel s Richard, Stretton, Sal, clerk to George Vaughan 14 Oct 1773
Wilkinson Anthony s Anthony, Bromley, miller to Nathaniel Gray, citizen and clothworker 9 Jul 1724
Wilkinson Francis s William, White Cross Street, turner to James Cotton, citizen and clothworker 9 Dec 1725 <14 Mar 1727/8 turned over by James' exec. to Daniel Rowles, citizen and haberdasher>
Williams Charles s Sarah, widow to Richard Smelt 13 Oct 1743 <9 Aug 1744 turned over to Robert Wrathall>
Williams Edward s Edward† to William Howes 12 May 1748
Williams James s John, St Thomas Southwark, Sry, victualler to Francis Wootton, citizen and haberdasher 12 Jul 1733
Williams John s Nicholas, Hinxworth, Hrt, yeoman† to John Blanfeild 1 Nov 1715 <free>
Williams Richard s John to John Jones 10 Nov 1763
Williams Thomas s Edward, Shrewsbury, Sal, farmer to John Taylor 16 Jan 1806
Willin William s Joseph to Thomas Emmery 14 Jan 1768 <9 Sep 1773 turned over to William Hayward>
Willis George s Richard to John Read 9 Feb 1769
Willis Joseph s John to Solomon Harris 8 Sep 1763
Willoughby John s John† to John Underwood 13 Jan 1742/3
Wilshire Jasper s Jasper, Hatfield, Hrt, gentleman† to George Long, cit. & blacksmith 6 Jan 1698/9
Wilson Charles s Edward to John Macartney 12 Jul 1753
Wilson George s John to David Taylor 9 Nov 1749
Wilson Richard s Richard to Thomas Grainger 14 Sep 1769
Wilson William s Robert, Atherstone, War, innholder to Walter Crew 10 Aug 1721
Wiltshire James s John, Biddestone, Wil, yeoman† to John Chapman 31 Mar 1806
Winch John s John, Southwark, Sry to Lionel Barnes 6 Jul 1714
Wine William s William, Mile End, Mdx, mariner to Joseph Johnson 14 Oct 1796
Winston Joseph s Thomas, cit. & clothworker to John French, cit. & currier 26 Apr 1700 <free>
Winter John s Thomas, Mdx, basketmaker to John Hill, citizen and goldsmith 11 May 1707 <free>
Winter John s Edward to William Goome 12 Apr 1753
Wise Samuel s Robert, Princes Street, Barbican, Mdx, wine cooper to Anthony Sparrow 23 Jan 1812
Wiseman John s Joshua, Chelsea, Mdx, gentleman† to James Huthwait, citizen and merchant tailor 22 Jun 1696 <free>
Witchet Charles Raymond s Luke, St Luke, Mdx, yeoman to Peter Duke 29 Feb 1816
Wohlman George s John Christian, Bridgewater Square, Mdx, yeoman to William Turner (jnr.) 10 May 1792
Wood James s John, Leather Lane, Holborn, Lnd, tailor to George Burnet 8 Dec 1785
Wood John s Ann, Red Cross Street, Lnd, widow to Nicholas Cunliffe 5 Dec 1721 <discharged - dead>
Wood John s ... to James William Hearne 6 Nov 1834
Wood Montague s Montague, Peterborough, Nth, innholder to John Dodsworth 11 Dec 1729
Wood Thomas s Thomas to Daniel Hammaker 11 Aug 1757
Wood Thomas s Edward, Golden Lane, St Giles Cripplegate, Mdx, bucklemaker† to John Miles 13 Feb 1783
Wood Thomas s Bartholomew, Plough Court, Barbican to Richard Sparrow 28 Nov 1825

GOLD AND SILVER WYRE DRAWERS' APPRENTICESHIPS

Wooding John s Henry, Eltham, Ken, yeoman to William Sympson 11 Jul 1734
Woodner John s John, Lnd, dyer to Edmund Sollers, citizen and merchant tailor 2 Jun 1713
 < 10 Nov 1718 turned over to William Simmons; free >
Wooley Isaac s Hugh† to John Underwood 9 Jun 1743 < 9 Aug 1744 turned over to
 Samuel Roberts >
Woolmore Daniel s Daniel to William Turner 14 Jul 1768 (charity of Cheshunt, Hrt)
Worsley James s John, Rivington, Lan, yeoman to Edward Hutchins, citizen and haberdasher
 7 Oct 1708 < free >
Worstick Somerset s William, Southminster, Ess, exciseman to Benjamin Jennings,
 citizen and grocer 14 Feb 1706/7
Worth Christopher s Richard, Whitechapel, Mdx, tallow chandler to Alexander Parrott,
 citizen and merchant tailor 1 Dec 1699 < free >
Wrathall Robert s Robert, citizen and innholder to Daniel Mallery 11 Oct 1716 < free >
Wright Charles s ..., Southwark, Sry to William Wright 16 Apr 1822
Wright John s Edmund, Hougham, Lin, gentleman† to Daniel Featley, citizen and merchant tailor
 23 Aug 1693
Wright John s Richard, citizen & turner to John Owen, cit. & longbowstringmaker 30 Aug 1693
Wright John s TM, Minories, Lnd† to William Read 10 Aug 1732
Wright William s William to James Norton 10 Sep 1789

Yates Robert s Robert, Hadley, Mdx, haberdasher† to Thomas Pensom, citizen and haberdasher
 21 May 1703
Yattes George s George to Samuel Roberts 13 Dec 1753 (premium paid by John Richardson)
York William s Edward, citizen & haberdasher to John Lane, cit. & weaver 23 Nov 1698 < free >
Young Charles s James, Covent Garden, Mdx, mercer to Walter Turner 25 Mar 1698
Young Samuel s William to John Macartney 9 Sep 1756
Young Samuel s William to ... Macartney .. ... 1764 < incomplete - 'not a binding' >
Young William s Benjamin, Spitalfields, Mdx, weaver to Nicholas Cunliffe 9 May 1734

INDEX OF MASTERS

[No surname given] Emery 11

Ailesbury Andrew 22
Alcraft *see* Allcraft
Aldred Samuel Botson 1
Allcraft (Alcraft) Henry 2, 22
Allen Joseph 11, 26
Alston (Alstone) Thomas 7, 9, 17, 24
Andrews Thomas Joseph 21
Appleford Henry Johnson 14, 24
Archer Peter 6
Ashmead John 4
Ashton Walter 16
Atherley Daniel 1, 2, 23
Atkins John 21; Joseph 22
Atkinson John 2, 15, 16, 23; Joseph 1, 8, 20; Thomas Pell 1
Atwood Thomas 1, 22
Aylesbury (Mr) 9; Andrew 9, 22, 23; Anna Maria 14; John 7

Bacon John 24, 25
Bailey (Baily) Mark 7, 9 (2), 11, 19, 23
Baker Thomas 18
Baldwin Humphrey 15, 26
Balsam William 20
Banks William 7, 16
Barnes Edward 19; John 7; Lionel 18, 21, 23, 27; William 3, 17, 23, 26
Barton Henry 7
Bassom William 12, 13, 15, 19 (2)
Batson John 17
Beer John 11
Bell James Thomas David 2
Bellinger Adam 12
Berkley John 3, 19; Robert 2, 7, 26
Berrisford Julius 25
Betteridge John 17, 24
Biddle Daniel 12
Birch (Burch) John 17; Richard 4, 5, 11, 13, 22, 24, 25, 27; Richard John 23; Thomas 8; Thomas Robert 2; William 14
Bird Richard 10; William 3, 16
Bishop Thomas 4
Blackwell John 4; Joseph 11, 26, 27
Blake Richard 3, 5, 24
Blanch Thomas 7, 8
Blandfield (Blanfeild) John 20, 27
Blatchford John 23
Blower Christopher 3
Booth James 6
Boston Samuel 15
Bowden Joseph 4, 15
Boyce Thomas 14, 17
Bracee (Bracey, Bracy) Thomas 8, 11, 12, 14, 25, 26
Brady Richard *see* vi
Brightwell Peter 17
Brock Thomas 1, 5 (2), 9, 11, 23, 24, 25

Brooksby Edward 4
Brown (Browne) Joseph 5, 12, 15 (2), 17, 19; Martha 20; Thomas 2, 14, 20, 23, 24
Bull Charles 4, 5, 21; William 4
Bullmore William 17
Burch *see* Birch
Burgesse William 6
Burgett Thomas 21
Burgin John 13, 23
Burnett (Burnet) George 2, 13, 21, 27; James 11, 18, 24; Sarah 9, 21
Burrell Mary 3, 15; William 11
Burrows John 3, 5, 16
Burton James 19; John 3, 8, 11 (2), 13, 23, 24; Joseph 24; Mary 11
Buswell Thomas 23
Butler Daniel 3 (2), 14; Nathaniel 24
Butter George 10

Cabell Francis 3, 8, 11, 18; Sarah 4, 7
Callis (Callisse, Collise) George 1, 11, 13, 22
Camroux Ferdinand Richard 11; John Lewis 8
Carter Joseph 2, 6, 9, 13, 16, 21
Cartwright William 9
Catling Martin 5
Chalmers John 5
Chamberlaine Joseph 9
Chandler Eleanor 10; Percival 8; Thomas 1, 10
Chapman John 8, 15, 18, 25, 27; Thomas 2, 5, 7, 9, 14, 17, 19, 25, 26
Chupsey John 3, 9, 13, 21
Churchman George 18; John 2 (2), 5 (2), 10, 11, 20, 21, 26
Clark Elizabeth 20
Clayton Susanna 18; William 14, 17, 21
Cluer Richard 7
Collins Daniel 10; John 1, 13; Philip 6; Thomas 1, 5, 11, 22
Collise *see* Callis
Cooke (Cook) John 6; Jonathan 25; Richard 1, 16, 20, 23
Cordrey John 10
Cotton James 27; William 16
Court John 22
Cowald Christopher 7, 13, 16, 26; Thomas 1, 4, 5, 12 (2), 14 (2), 16, 18, 19, 20, 24, 26
Cowley William 9, 13
Cox Robert 19
Crew Robert 2, 8, 9, 10 (3), 19, 20 (2), 22; Walter 4, 13, 17 (3), 19, 27
Crooke James 3
Crouch Samuel 6, 12 (2), 13 (2), 16, 22; Stephen 2, 8, 10, 12, 13, 17, 18, 26
Cumberledge (Cumberlidge) John 10, 16
Cunliffe (Mr) 2; Nicholas 1, 10, 14 (2), 16, 18, 21, 23, 27, 28
Currier Thomas 5

Dandridg William 26

INDEX OF MASTERS

Dark William 1
Davis (Davies) Edward 3, 7, 13, 18, 22 (3), 27; Elizabeth 6, 20
Dawkins John 15, 22; Samuel 21
Dawson Thomas 13
Day Daniel 23; John 6; Jonathan 17
Dayles John 8
Deeves Henry 3, 22, 26
de Medina *see* Medina
Dennis Charles 14; Edward 5; James 4 (2), 8, 11, 13, 17 (2), 18, 19, 22, 24 *and see* vi; Thomas 8
Dodsworth Charles 1; John 4, 7, 9, 19, 20, 24, 26, 27
Dormer (Dormar) Ralph 4, 8
Doughty Michael 13, 18, 19, 22
Douglas James 2 (2), 3, 7, 8 (2), 9, 10, 21
Dracutt William 18
Drake John 1, 20
Drury Richard 1, 2 (2), 9, 13 (2), 15, 22, 25 *and see* vi
Duffeild John 12, 16
Duke Peter 4, 10, 16 (4), 27
Dunne John 1

Eamonson Joshua 10
Edenbury George 7, 14; John 1, 11, 24
Ederingham Ann 20
Edwards Edward 5, 16, 18 (2), 23; John 5, 18; Mary 6, 18, 21; Thomas 2
Embry John 9, 24
Emmery Thomas 27
Estwick Nathaniel 12
Etherington Thomas 8
Evans John 11; Robert 9; William 23
Everett Joseph 9, 19, 26, 27

Farr John 2, 20; William 26
Farrow *see* Pharrow
Featley Daniel 15, 28
Fenton Samuel 23
Ferris (Ferrys) John 1, 9
Field Arabella 7, 18, 24
Finch Edward 6, 21; John 3
Fisher Daniel 8, 14
Fletcher John 2, 18
Ford John 10, 20, 23
Fowler James 6; Jonathan 17
Franklyn Thomas 19
French George 10; John 21, 27
Frouchon John 10

Ganton (Gantom, Gantum) Elizabeth 1; John 20; William 6
Gardner (Gardiner) John 5, 10; Thomas 5, 20, 22
Gascoyne (Gascoine) (Mrs) 4; Elizabeth 2, 7, 21; Robert 18, 21, 27; Susanna 12; William 3 (2), 23, 25

Gibbon Robert 11, 12, 14
Gifford John 1, 8, 13, 16, 19, 20, 23
Glyde Robert 4, 6, 11, 16, 20, 21, 26
Godwyn Thomas 10
Goff (Goffe) Benjamin 8, 22
Goodchild Robert 19
Goome Stephen 10, 15; William 2 (3), 12, 16 (3), 18, 22, 23, 26, 27
Grainger Thomas 13, 18 (2), 27
Grammer (Gramar) James 1, 6
Granger Thomas 11
Gray Nathaniel 27
Green (Greene) Francis 11, 25; John 4, 5, 6, 8 (2), 9, 10, 11, 22, 25; Pauncefoot 7, 14, 15, 20
Greenwood William 15
Gregory Joseph 6
Grenway Richard 25
Gutteridge ... 17; William 3, 6, 9 (2), 12, 13, 17, 18, 19, 20, 23

Hales Edward 9, 14, 24
Hammacker (Hammaker) Daniel 15, 27
Hammond (Hamond) John 14, 15, 19; Peter 12, 25; Sarah 12
Handy William 11
Harker William 1 (2), 2 (2), 18, 21, 24 (2), 25
Harrington Joseph 12, 13, 18
Harris Benjamin 11, 12, 18; Elizabeth 3, 8, 12; Solomon 5 (2), 19, 27
Hart Moses 6; William 19
Haynes John 8
Hayward (Haywood) Joseph 2; William 27
Hearne (Herne) James William 8, 10, 27; William 12
Heathcote Michael 19
Hemmett William 14, 15, 17
Herne *see* Hearne
Hewes *see* Hughes
Hill (Hills) George 12; John 10, 27; Richard 1, 19, 21; Roger 12, 20
Hooper William 18
Hosier Charles 6
Houlton Francis 2, 6, 13, 15, 26
How Catherine 3, 11; Daniel 5, 7 (2), 8, 11, 15, 16, 17 (2), 24, 26
Howes William 21, 27
Hudson Henry 15
Hughes (Hewes, Hughs) Edward 12, 16, 19, 21, 23, 24, 25; John 4, 12, 14, 15, 22 (2), 23; William 7, 25
Hurst Lewis 14
Hussey Robert 12, 13
Hutchins Edward 28
Huthwait (Huthwait) James 12, 14, 27

Isles Marmaduke 5

Jacob Joseph 18

INDEX OF MASTERS

James William 14
Jellico Andrew 2
Jennings Benjamin 26, 28
Jephcoate (Jephcaute) William 17, 26
Johnson Henry 14; Henry William 11, 13, 14; Joseph 3, 6, 7, 9, 12, 15, 21, 27
Jones John 1, 3, 4, 10, 27; Robert 17
Joseph (Josephs) John 2, 5, 24; Susanna 20

Kilpin Joseph 11, 19
King Richard 14

Lane John 6, 22, 25, 28; Nathaniel 24
Langdell Edward 4
Langdon (Langden) Edward 4, 13, 15, 18, 19, 20, 23, 24; John 20
Laxton James 7, 9, 15, 20, 21; Martin 19
Leaver Edward 15
Leech John 1 *and see* vi
Lewis William 16
Littlewood Richard 6, 12, 20
Lockwood Charles 2, 11, 14, 16
Long George 27
Longden Robert 15, 21; Roger 12
Lovelace Henry 24
Lowther Richard 14, 25

Macartney (Maccartney) ... 28; John 11, 15, 17, 18, 19, 27 (2), 28
McClary Samuel 16
McDonald William 4
Macey John 2, 3, 16, 19, 24
Maddey (Mady) John 14, 24
Mallory (Mallery) Daniel 6, 16 (2), 17, 25, 28
Marlow John 13
Marriott Thomas 6
Marshall Samuel 5, 14
Martin George 5; John 6; Thomas 16, 22; William Corneck 5
Matthews (Mathew) Charles 18; Thomas 26
May John 2, 6, 17
Mayor John 5
Meakins George 8 *and see* vi
Medina Ferdinand de 5
Miflin Richard 18
Miles John 4, 24, 27; Lewis 22, 23; Lewis Charles 24
Millist James 7
Mole Thomas 13, 24
Moore (More) Peter 7, 20
Morgan William 1, 19, 22
Morris Samuel 3
Mothram (Mottrom) Edward 7, 17 (2)
Munt John 16; (Mr) 5

Naylor George 3, 4, 8, 12, 17, 21; George William 2
Neal (Neale, Neall) Robert 4, 7, 9, 17, 19, 22, 23

Negus Benjamin 10 (2), 13, 24
Newport George 8
Newton Thomas 1, 19
Norman Anthony 25
Norton James 10, 28
Nott Edward 6

Osborne John 11; William 22
Owen John 8, 13, 18, 28

Page Edward 16, 21
Palmer Isaac 13
Panton Richard 4
Parkins Elizabeth 21
Parratt (Parrott) Alexander 2, 19, 28; James 9, 24
Paxton Ezekias 22; Michael 2
Pearsall William 18
Pensom Thomas 2, 3, 5, 28
Percival Samuel 25
Perkins Thomas 19
Pert Thomas 17, 19; Walter 2
Pharrow Samuel 6
Pierpoynt Thomas 17
Pilgrim John 25
Pingstone Nicholas 1
Pitcher (Pitchers) Thomas 8, 12, 15, 19, 20, 23, 25, 26
Pitter Robert 2, 13, 24
Pope John 6
Potter Caleb 15
Price Mathew 6; Thomas 2
Prosser (Mr) 5; Thomas 6, 7, 25, 26
Proudley John 4, 7
Pugh Richard 10, 12, 14, 21

Quarry Orme 2, 8, 14
Questead (Questeard, Quested) Henry 1, 2, 4, 6, 9, 21 (3), 22; Mary 21
Questwood Robert 1, 22

Read John 1, 4, 7, 8, 11, 12 (3), 13, 25, 27; Mary 6, 17; Samuel 7; Samuel Fenton 7, 11; William 4, 8 (2), 9, 11, 14, 20, 22, 24, 28
Reeve (Reeves) John 20, 24; Thomas 22; William 14, 26
Reynolds James 1, 8; Robert 3, 9, 16
Richardson John 4 (2), 10, 14 (2), 15, 23, 28
Richmond Oliver 10
Rivers (Riviers) George 15, 17; Henry 8, 9, 17
Roberts Benjamin 1, 3, 5, 16, 17, 19, 23, 25; Noah 6, 11, 26; Richard 16, 20; Samuel 1, 3, 4, 6, 9, 10, 11 (2), 16, 27, 28; Stephen 22
Rowles Daniel 27
Rugby William 15, 18
Russell (Russel, Russle) Benjamin 8, 15, 18, 22, 26

INDEX OF MASTERS

Rutland James 14, 20

Salmon John 9
Salter Richard 24
Sansum William 5, 7, 17, 23
Saunders Robert 9; William 19
Scarnell John 7, 8, 14, 18
Scatliff Henry 12
Scott Charles 3, 9; Hewson 3, 13, 21
Scovell James 4, 11 (2), 17, 26
Sedgewick George 16
Sewell George 3, 9, 13, 15; Robert 15
Shaler John 7, 9
Sharpe Thomas 10, 22
Shaw William 5, 18, 22, 23
Shepperd Philip 22
Shirley Richard 18
Shovell (Shovel) Sarah 26; Thomas 6 (2), 17, 25, 26
Simmonds (Simmons, Symonds, Symons) William 3, 16, 21, 28
Simpson (Sympson) Luke 3; Mary 9, 14, 15, 24; Thomas 8; William 15, 17, 19 (2), 20, 23, 28
Slane William 15
Smelt Richard 7, 12, 20 (2), 26, 27
Smith John 1, 3, 13; Joyce 17; Mary 17, 23; Mary widow of John 11; Nathaniel 22
Snow John 22; Richard 13
Sollers Edmund 9, 28
Southouse Henry 1, 15; William 20, 23
Sparrow Anthony 2, 22, 23 (3), 25 (2), 26, 27; Henry 10, 23; Richard 27; Simon 23
Spearing George 12
Sproston Samuel 20
Spurr Joseph 20
Stackhouse William 4 (2), 18, 19, 21, 27
Stanton John 9, 18
Stilwell Edward 8, 20
Strong David 22; John 3
Studdard John 3, 22
Sturley Richard 8, 12, 13
Swaine John 1
Sweeting Jonathan 11, 12, 23; Mary 7
Swepson William 17
Symonds, Symons *see* Simmons
Sympson *see* Simpson

Tanner Edmund 17
Tatum Thomas 24, 25
Taunton Thomas 14
Taylor (Tayler) David 4, 6, 11, 17, 18, 24, 27; John 10 (3), 19, 27; Richard 13, 19, 22, 25
Thame Thomas 13
Thomas William 2
Townsend George 4, 14, 24
Tozer Richard 26
Truscoat George 8

Tucker Joseph 3 (2), 4, 5, 6, 7, 8, 12, 15, 22, 25, 26
Turberville George 7
Turner ... 11, 12; Edward 8; Henry 21; James 12, 19; John 4, 10, 11, 22; Walter 8, 16, 20, 25, 28; William 4, 5, 7, 8, 19, 21, 23, 25 (3), 27, 28
Tuthill Richard 10

Underwood Charles 21; John 8, 10, 12, 25, 27, 28

Vaughan George 15 (2), 27

Wagstaffe (Wagstaff) Thomas 4, 5, 10, 11
Wainwright John 10, 21
Wale John 16
Walker William 1, 18
Walklate John 7, 8 (2), 9, 11, 24
Waller John 2, 3, 10, 13, 15, 20, 21
Walter John 6
Walton Jeremiah 25; William 14
Wasburne Philip 13
Washbourn Goodwin 2
Washbourne (Wasburne, Washbourn, Washburn, Wasshburn) Goodwin 2, 5, 12; Philip 13, 26 (2); Thomas 21
Watkin John 6
Watts George Edward 26
Webb ... 9
Weldon Charles 14
Wells Thomas 1, 5
Wellsborne John 15
Wenham Warner 24
Wescott John 26
Wheatly James 26
Whilton John 26
Whinnell John 6, 10 (2), 16, 17, 25
White James 3, 5, 21; Thomas 5
Wigginton William King 16
Wilkinson Francis 2, 4, 18, 22, 24
Williams William 3
Willin Robert 23
Wilshire (Wiltshire) Jasper 13, 21
Winston (Winstone) Catherine 20; Thomas 4, 7
Winter John 2, 4 (2), 7 (2), 11, 16; Wandell 6, 18
Wohlman George 3
Wood Joseph 26; Walter 2
Wootton Francis 6, 7, 14, 27
Worsley Evan 1; Evans 2; James 10
Wotton Francis 8
Wrathall (Mr) 11; Richard 6; Robert 1, 7, 8, 16, 18, 21, 22, 26, 27 *and see* vi
Wright William 28
Wybourne (Wybourn) George 16, 17 (2), 24

York William 15

INDEX OF PLACES

UNIDENTIFIED COUNTY

Bromley 27

ABROAD

Man, Isle of
    Castle Town 26

BEDFORDSHIRE 9

Apsley 9
Bedford 15
Dunstable 3
Gravenhurst 2
Keysoe 23
Market Street 13
Maulden 25
Shefford 20
Toddington 24

BERKSHIRE

Buckland
    Carswell Marsh 13
Hagborne 6
Reading
    St Lawrence 4 (2), 5
Windsor 14, 19, 25
Wokingham 13

BUCKINGHAMSHIRE 15

Botolph Claydon 10
Great Brickhill 2
Great Horwood 26
Iver 3
Newport Pagnell 16
Shipton 9
Soulbury 5
Stony Stratford 3, 15
Stow 22
Sulham Bannister 5
Waddenham 6
Whaddon 12, 17, 18
Woburn 23
Wycombe 8
    High Wycombe 13

CAMBRIDGESHIRE

Wicken 9

CHESHIRE

Carrington 9
Knutsford 20
Taxal 12

DERBYSHIRE

Boyleston 1
Whittington 10
Wingfield Manor 12
Wormhill 16

DEVONSHIRE

Exeter 23
    near Exeter 9

DORSET

Bridport 27
Lyme 18
Marnhull 20

DURHAM

Barnards Castle 24
Durham 17

ESSEX

Barking 1
Broxted 10
Coggeshall 6, 24
Cranham 18
Dagenham 17
Hornchurch 24
Kelvedon 24
Moreton 26
Pleshey 15
Southminster 28
Stratford Langthorne 7
Thaxted 21
Theydon Bois 10
Walthamstow 24

GLOUCESTERSHIRE

Bristol 3, 12, 24
Charlton Abbots 1
Cheltenham 26
Gloucester 8
Lydney 8
Mitcheldean 25
Newent 18
Painswick 10
Rodborough 21
Stow 6
Stroud 26
Tewkesbury 12
Wotton under Edge 7, 10, 19 (2), 20

INDEX OF PLACES

HAMPSHIRE

Basingstoke 6
Christ Church 26
Crawley 20
Gosport 19
Hamble 4
Overton 3
Portsmouth 25
Southampton 22
Sparsholt 12

HEREFORDSHIRE 11

Delamare 25
Leominster 4
Madley 26
Much Cowarne 5

HERTFORDSHIRE

Ashwell 20
Benington 19
Cheshunt 4, 5, 13, 25, 26, 28
Digswell 18
Hatfield 27
Hertford 20
Hinxworth 27
Hitchin 11
St Albans 19
Stanstead Abbots 18
Watford 23

HUNTINGDONSHIRE

Huntingdon 20

IRELAND

Dublin 5, 25

KENT

Canterbury 2
Eltham 28
Greenwich 23
Maidstone 20
Ramsgate 16
St Mary Cray 26
Sevenoaks 1
Sundridge 1
Woolwich 10, 12

LANCASHIRE

Accrington 7
Hall Sefton 18
Lathom 17

LANCASHIRE [continued]

Maghull 15
Rivington 28

LEICESTERSHIRE

Great ... 8

LINCOLNSHIRE

Carrington 9
Grantham 6
Hougham 28
Stamford 14

LONDON/MIDDLESEX

All Hallows London Wall 2
All Hallows Staining 18
Bethnal Green 2, 12, 16, 21, 23
Blackfriars, Earl Street 26
Bloomsbury 7, 21, 25
    Bloomsbury Market 22
Blow Bladder Street 20
Brentford 22
Bromley St Leonard 6
Brooks Market 14
Bucklersbury 5
Chelsea 4, 8, 14, 21, 25, 27
Clerkenwell 1 (2), 3, 11, 17, 19, 23 (3), 24, 27
    Clerkenwell Green 23
    St James 3, 8 (2), 11
    St John 12
    St John Street 2
    St John's Court 13
Crooked Lane 23
Doctors Commons 24
Edmonton 11, 17
Enfield 21
East Smithfield 8
Finchley
    Whetstone 5, 14
Fleet Ditch 19
Fleet Street 2, 7
Fore Street 7, 22, 23
Grays Inn 8
Grosvenor Street 15
Hackney 11
Hadley 12, 28
Hammersmith 1
Hampton
    Hampton Court 2
Hendon 8, 17
Holborn 1 (2), 3, 7, 14, 17, 18, 19, 25, 26
    Chapel Street, Bedford Row 3
    Grays Inn 8
    Grays Inn Lane 14

INDEX OF PLACES

LONDON/MIDDLESEX [*continued*]

Holborn [*continued*]
    Hatton Garden 14 (2)
    High Holborn 10
    Kirby Street 25
    Leather Lane 11, 27
    Shoe Lane 23
Hornsey 13
    Highgate 15
Huggin Lane 3
Islington 6, 14, 27
Jewin Street 6, 9
London 9
Kensington 25
Limehouse 10
Long Alley 10
Middlesex 4, 6, 8, 19, 22
Minories 26, 28
New Street 7
Newgate Street 22
Nightingale Lane 4
Norton Folgate 6, 17
Philip Lane, London Wall 7
Poor Jury Lane 25
Poplar 11
Pouls Alley 23
Puddle Dock 17
Queenhithe 6
Red Cross Street 11, 13, 15, 17, 22, 27
Ruislip 16, 19
St Andrew 18
St Andrew Undershaft 7
St Bartholomew the Great
    Cloth Fair 19
St Bartholomew the Less 5
St Botolph Aldersgate 3, 7, 8, 11, 13, 17, 23
    Aldersgate 19
    Aldersgate Street 3, 10, 20, 23 (2)
        Crown Court 12
    Falcon Street 13
    Glasshouse Yard 6
    Little Britain 7, 8
St Botolph Aldgate 14, 20
    Aldgate 1, 16, 23
    Chequer Alley 16
    Petticoat Lane 9, 22
St Botolph Bishopsgate
    Bishopsgate Street, Dunings Alley 22
St Bride 15, 23
St Dunstan in the West 5, 14, 19
    Fetter Lane 9, 27
St Faith 15
St George in the East 1
St Giles Cripplegate 2 (3), 4 (3), 6, 9, 10 (2), 11 (2), 13, 15 (3), 17, 21 (3), 24 (2), 25 (3), 26 (3)

LONDON/MIDDLESEX [*continued*]

St Giles Cripplegate [*continued*]
    Barbican 19, 24
    Beech Lane 1, 11
    Bell Alley 8
    Bridgewater Square 8, 27
    Cripplegate 16, 20
    Crowderswell Alley 22
    Golden Lane 3, 12, 23, 27
    Grub Street 6, 8, 9, 10, 13, 17, 22 (2), 26
    Moor Lane 6, 27
    Plough Court, Barbican 27
    Princes Street, Barbican 27
St Giles in the Fields 6, 14, 18, 19, 22, 23
    Wild Street 8
St James Garlickhythe 12
St Luke 1, 2, 4, 8, 12 (2), 17, 18, 20, 21, 27
    Bell Alley, Goswell Street 16
    Bunhill Row 22
    Old Street 24
    Old Street Road 12
    White Cross Street 1 (2), 5, 6, 7, 9 (2), 11 (2), 14, 16, 18, 19, 22, 25, 26 (2), 27
St Margaret Pattens 21
St Mary Axe 22
St Marylebone 18
    Bond Street 16
    South Audley Street 6
St Olave Hart Street
    Crutched Friars 5
St Pancras
    Kentish Town 4
St Pauls Churchyard 2
St Sepulchre 5, 21, 24, 25
    Benjamin Street, Cow Cross 8
    Charterhouse Lane 3
    Chick Lane 7, 24
    Cow Cross 3
    Ditchside 13
    Sharps Alley, Smithfield 1
St Stephen Coleman Street
    Coleman Street 14
    Great Swan Alley, Coleman Street 17
    Swan Alley 4
Shadwell 21
    Labour in Vain Court 18, 21
Silver Street, Wood Street 4
Shoreditch 2, 4, 5, 7, 9, 10, 11, 13, 14 (2), 15, 16, 18, 21, 24
    Holywell Mount 9
    Hoxton 13
Spitalfields 4, 7, 8, 9, 17, 19, 21, 22, 24, 28
Stepney 6, 10, 16
    Commercial Road 10
    Mile End 27

INDEX OF PLACES

LONDON/MIDDLESEX [*continued*]

Stepney [*continued*]
   Ratcliff 16
   Ratcliff Cross 13
   Richard Street, Commercial Road 19
Stoke Newington 8
Stratford le Bow 13
   Bow 7, 24
Thames Street 2, 4
Turnbell Street 3
Tottenham 1, 18
Tower Street 20
Twickenham 13
Wapping 4, 10, 17, 19
   New Crane 1
West Smithfield 1
Westminster 1, 11, 12, 13, 15, 16 (2), 18
   Covent Garden 16, 24, 28
      Bedford Street 11
      Maiden Lane 12
   Pye Street 17
   St Ann (Soho) 6
   St Clement Danes 2, 14
   St George Hanover Square 14
      Pimlico 10, 23
   St James Westminster 9, 13, 15
      Brewer Street 7
      Petty France 11
      Tyler Street 10
   St John Westminster 21
      Marsham Street 14
   St Margaret Westminster 3, 12, 17
   St Martin in the Fields 3 (2), 5, 6, 10 (2), 14, 16, 20, 22, 23, 25, 26
      Drury Lane 23
      Dukes Court, St Martins Lane 26
      Hewitts Court, Charing Cross 2
      Leg Alley, Long Acre 25
   Scotland Yard 16
   Strand 14, 21
      Hungerford Market 2
      Vine Street 25
Whitefriars 17
Windmill Hill 12
Whitechapel 2, 7, 14, 19, 28
   Goodmans Fields 25
Willesden 25

NORFOLK

Kings Lynn 17
New Walsingham 11
Thetford 22

NORTHAMPTONSHIRE

Apethorpe 3
Cosgrove 5
   Old Stratford 15
Deene 3
Gretton 8
Kettering 20
Newnham 12
Peterborough 27
Wollaston 12
Woodford 5

NORTHUMBERLAND 21

Blankinsopp Castle 3
Newcastle on Tyne 16
Shields 22
Wooler 6

NOTTINGHAMSHIRE

East Markham 9
Nottingham 14

OXFORDSHIRE

Banbury 11
Barton 14
Bicester 4
Charlbury 12
Nuffield 11
Witney 27
Woodstock 12
   New Woodstock 12

RUTLAND

Glaston 9

SHROPSHIRE

Bodwell 17
Houlditch Woolsington 2
Shrewsbury 6, 10, 15, 22, 27
Stretton 27
Wem 15, 16
Woolascott 19

SCOTLAND

Edinburgh 17, 19

SOMERSET

Barton 10
Bristol 19
Charlton Adam 10

INDEX OF PLACES

SOMERSET [*continued*]

Frome 24
Mells 1
Stoke 10
Taunton 9
Wells 13
Wookey 10

STAFFORDSHIRE 24

Elford 18

SUFFOLK

Clo... 13
Edwardstone 10
Graunton 5
Groton 10
Ipswich 17
Nayland 17
Sudbury 22

SURREY

Battersea 14
Bermondsey 4, 10 (3), 13, 24, 26
Bookham 13
Byfleet 16
Chaldon 17
Chipstead 15
Clapham 12
Croydon 2
Effingham 2
Epsom 3
Godstone 4
Guildford 8
Lambeth 4, 8, 9, 14, 15, 17 (2), 18
Mortlake 12
Newington 8, 26
    Newington Green 8
    Suffolk Street, East Blackman Street 26
    Walworth 12
Richmond 20
Rotherhithe 6, 22
Southwark 3, 7, 8, 11, 16, 19, 22, 23, 27, 28
    Castle Lane 24
    St John Horsleydown 11
    St Mary Overy 4, 20
    St Olave Southwark 1, 18
    St Saviour Southwark 2, 5
    St Thomas Southwark 27
    Snows Fields 14
    Tooley Street 25

SUSSEX

East Grinstead 24
Storrington 20

WALES

Bangor, Denbighshire 13, 24
Llanmerewig, Montgomeryshire 7
Montgomeryshire 20
Pembrokeshire 10
Sandiston, Caernarvonshire 21
Wrexham, Denbighshire 13

WARWICKSHIRE

Atherstone 1, 27
Birmingham 8
Coleshill 26
Coventry 14
Halford 8
Kenilworth 16
Stratford on Avon 9
Stretton 9
Temple Tysoe 17
Warwick 6, 16

WILTSHIRE

Biddestone 27
Chippenham 23
Devizes 21
Malmesbury 9
Salisbury 24
Urchfont 4

WORCESTERSHIRE

Pirton 13
Stoke Prior 19
Wick 22
Worcester 1, 3
    St Nicholas 21

YORKSHIRE

Appleton le Moors 20
Bedale 20, 23
Fringill 20
Hutton le Hole 26
Stokesley 20

INDEX OF SUBJECTS

apothecary 3, 5, 6, 15, 16
   citizen and apothecary 3
armourer
   citizen and armourer 3, 14, 22

baker 3, 10 (2), 14, 17, 18, 24
barber 7, 11, 14 (3), 15, 16, 23
   chirurgeon 19
   citizen and barber surgeon 1
   perukemaker 7, 13
basketmaker 27
bedsteadmaker 7
bitmaker 23
blacksmith 12, 15, 19
   citizen and blacksmith 4 (2), 5 (2), 6 (2), 7, 10 (2), 11, 12 (3), 15 (2), 17 (2), 18 (3), 20 (3), 24 (4), 25, 26 (2), 27
   smith 1, 5, 16, 26
blanket maker 27
blockmaker 17
bookbinder 1
bookseller
   hatter and bookseller 26
brandy seller 9
brazier 13, 16
brewer 22, 25
   citizen and brewer 4
bricklayer 1, 5, 26, 27
broderer
   citizen and broderer 1 (2), 11, 18, 22
brushmaker 21
bucklemaker 27
butcher 4, 14, 15, 20
buttonhole turner 9

cabinet maker 2, 6, 24
calico printer 6
carman 13, 23
carpenter 1, 3, 8 (2), 11, 12, 13, 14, 18 (2), 19, 25
   citizen and carpenter 5, 22
carrier 20
carver
   carver and gilder 7
   stone carver 14
chairmaker 24
   cane chairmaker 2
chandler 21
   citizen and tallow chandler 11
   citizen and wax chandler 4, 15
   tallow chandler 10, 13, 28
cheesemonger 10
chirurgeon 19
chocolate maker 3
clergymen
   clerk 1, 5, 10, 11 (2), 13, 15, 17, 18, 20, 27
   dissenting minister 13

clergymen [*continued*]
   protestant dissenting minister 13
   rector 15
clothier 1, 12, 20, 21, 24, 26
clothworker 7, 10, 20 (2), 25, 26
   citizen and clothworker 4, 5, 7, 27
coachmaker
   citizen and coachmaker 8, 9
   coach painter 15
coachman 3 (2), 7, 11
collarmaker 17
commercial agent 17
compass maker 22
cook 18
   citizen and cook 19
cooper 4, 12, 17, 19 (2), 21
   citizen and cooper 7, 16, 21
   wine cooper 15, 27
coppersmith 27
cordwainer 1 (2), 2, 8, 10, 14 (2), 19 (3), 20, 21
   citizen and cordwainer 1, 2, 4 (2), 5, 6, 7, 8, 10, 12, 13, 14, 15 (2), 16, 17, 18, 19 (2), 20 (3), 23 (2), 24
currier
   citizen and currier 21, 27
cutler 8, 23
   citizen and cutler 1

distiller 1, 15, 19
doctor of physic 23
draper 6, 20
   citizen and draper 14
   linen draper 9, 14
dyer 20
   citizen and dyer 1, 2 (2), 20
   silk dyer 10, 22

esquire 3, 6
exciseman 28

factor
   tea factor 6
farmer 13, 14, 27
farrier 2, 25, 26
   citizen and farrier 16
fellmonger 4
feltmaker
   citizen and feltmaker 21
fisherman 20
fishmonger 10
   citizen and fishmonger 5 (2), 10, 20, 21, 22
flatter 13
flaxdresser 13
fletcher
   citizen and fletcher 9

INDEX OF SUBJECTS

founder 23
    brass founder 12, 19
    citizen and founder 8
frameworkknitter
    citizen and stocking frameworkknitter 18
    stocking frameworkknitter 20

gardener 1, 12, 13, 15, 20, 25, 26
gentleman 1 (2), 2 (4), 3, 4, 5, 6 (3), 7, 8 (3), 9 (3), 10, 12 (4), 14, 15, 16 (4), 17 (2), 18 (2), 19 (3), 20 (3), 21 (4), 22 (2), 23, 24, 25 (3), 26, 27 (2), 28
gilder 10
girdler
    citizen and girdler 10, 15
glass
    glass cutter 6, 23
    glass scalloper 8
    glassmaker 11
    glazier 3, 9, 22
glover 4, 19, 25, 26
    citizen and glover 9, 14, 18
goldsmith 6, 11 (2), 12
    citizen and goldsmith 1 (2), 2, 4, 5, 6 (5), 10 (4), 11, 14 (2), 15 (3), 16 (3), 18, 19 (2), 20, 21 (2), 22 (2), 23 (6), 24, 25, 27
grazier 10
greengrocer 9
grocer 5, 13, 18, 22, 24, 25
    citizen and grocer 2 (2), 7, 8, 9 (2), 11, 12, 14, 16, 18, 22, 25, 26 (2), 28
gunner
    master gunner 12
gunsmith 7, 14, 20, 26

haberdasher 14, 16, 18, 19, 28
    citizen and haberdasher 1 (3), 2 (2), 3 (4), 4, 5, 6 (2), 7, 8, 11, 13, 14 (2), 16, 17, 18, 19 (3), 21 (3), 22 (2), 24, 26, 27 (3), 28
hats
    citizen and hatbandmaker 2
    hatbandmaker 12, 18
    hatter 19, 21
    hatter and bookseller 26
hempdresser 14, 26
husbandman 9, 12, 14, 16, 24, 27

innholder 2, 7, 9, 15, 23, 27
    citizen and innholder 14, 28
ironmonger 2, 9, 18
    citizen and ironmonger 9, 25

jeweller 2, 24, 25
joiner 3, 15
    citizen and joiner 12, 19, 24, 26

labourer 2 (2), 3 (2), 4 (2), 5, 6, 7, 8 (5), 9, 11, 14, 15 (2), 16 (2), 17, 18 (2), 19, 20 (2), 21 (3), 22, 23, 24 (5), 26, 27
laceman 7
lapidary 3
leatherdresser 8
leatherseller
    citizen and leatherseller 16, 22
locksmith 1
longbowstringmaker
    citizen and longbowstringmaker 1, 2, 3, 5, 6, 8 (2), 9 (3), 12 (2), 13 (4), 16, 17 (3), 18 (2), 19, 20, 22, 23 (2), 24 (4), 25 (3), 26 (3), 28
loriner
    citizen and loriner 7

maltster 9, 24
mariner 4 (2), 7, 10, 12, 16, 17, 18, 21 (2), 22 (2), 26, 27
mason 24
    citizen and mason 2
    stonemason 13, 15
mathematical instrument maker 6
mercer 11, 20, 22, 26, 28
    citizen and mercer 23
merchant 6, 25
    coal merchant 17
    merchant tailor *see* tailor
    wine merchant 23
miller 27
milliner 2, 25

needlemaker 9

ostler 3

packer
    citizen and packer 7
painter 14, 22, 23
    coach painter 15
pensioner 8
perukemaker 7, 13
pewterer
    citizen and pewterer 10, 19
pipemaker 11
plasterer
    citizen and plasterer 7
plumber 12, 13
    citizen and plumber 13, 25
porter 15, 18, 21
potter 14
poulterer 15

refiner 13
ropemaker 10 (2), 19, 22, 24
rust splitter 12

INDEX OF SUBJECTS

saddler 5, 26
salter
    citizen and salter 9
sawyer 11, 13, 17, 18, 27
scrivener 13
    citizen and scrivener 3, 11, 12, 13, 18, 25
sergemaker 5
shipwright 4, 11
    citizen and shipwright 10
shoemaker 2, 6 (3), 13, 16, 17, 18, 21, 24 (2), 25
silk throster
    citizen and silk throster 10
silversmith 12
smith 1, 5, 16, 26
spinner 1, 20, 25
stablekeeper 3
stationer 20
    citizen and stationer 10, 23
staymaker 6, 19
stocking frameworkknitter 20
    citizen and stocking frameworkknitter 18
stonemason 13, 15
surgeon 1, 6, 13, 15, 22
sweep 9

tailor 1, 2, 3 (3), 5 (2), 7, 8, 10, 12, 13 (2), 14 (2), 15, 17 (2), 20 (2), 21, 22, 23 (4), 24, 26, 27
    citizen and merchant tailor 1 (4), 2 (2), 3 (4), 4, 5 (2), 6 (3), 7 (4), 9 (3), 10 (3), 11 (4), 12 (5), 13 (5), 14 (4), 15 (2), 19 (3), 20 (3), 22 (2), 23 (2), 24 (4), 25 (2), 26 (2), 27, 28
tanner 1, 13
tide waiter 23
tinplateworker 2

toymaker 4
transported 27
turner 4
    buttonhole turner 9
    citizen and turner 7, 19, 25, 26 (2), 28

victualler 1, 4, 8 (2), 9, 22, 25 (2), 27
vintner 4, 7, 8, 11
    citizen and vintner 2 (2), 6, 7, 8 (2), 14, 19, 21, 23

watches
    watch chainmaker 4
    watchcasemaker 25
    watchmaker 12, 22, 24, 27
waterman 6, 10, 12, 14, 17 (2), 22
wax chandler
    citizen and wax chandler 4, 15
weaver 5, 6, 7, 9 (2), 10 (4), 12 (2), 17, 19, 22 (3), 23 (2), 26, 28
    citizen and weaver 1 (2), 3 (2), 6 (2), 7 (2), 8 (2), 11 (2), 12 (2), 13, 15, 17, 18, 20, 21 (2), 22 (2), 23, 25 (2), 26 (3), 28
    engine weaver 23
wheelwright 1, 4, 6, 25
    citizen and wheelwright 7
whitesmith 3
wiredrawer 4, 8, 17, 21, 25
woolcomber 17, 26

yeoman 1 (4), 2 (6), 3 (3), 4 (2), 5 (4), 6 (2), 7 (3), 8 (4), 9 (8), 10 (6), 11 (5), 12 (4), 13 (2), 14, 16 (5), 17 (4), 18 (4), 19, 20 (2), 21 (2), 22 (3), 23 (3), 24 (5), 25 (4), 26 (4), 27 (4), 28